At thirty-six Marilyn Jensen, the mother of three children, found herself divorced and on her own for the first time in her life. In *Formerly Married,* the current Book Editor of *Guideposts* has combined her own experiences with the insights of other widowed and divorced women to present a warm, sympathetic and practical look at life from the point of view of the housewife and mother whose marriage has just ended.

Formerly Married contains practical advice on overcoming grief . . . coping with feelings of embarrassment, guilt, anger, failure . . . making a living . . . finding new friends . . . searching for a substitute mate . . . seeking professional counseling . . . single parenting . . . making decisions . . . learning to enjoy yourself . . . It is an invaluable resource for anyone whose marriage has come to an end and who wants to make a new beginning.

Learning To Live With Yourself Formerly Married

Marilyn Jensen

A JOVE BOOK

This Jove book contains the complete
text of the original hardcover edition.
It has been completely reset in a typeface
designed for easy reading, and was printed
from new film.

FORMERLY MARRIED

A Jove Book / published by arrangement with
Westminster Press

PRINTING HISTORY
Westminster Press edition published 1983
Jove edition / April 1984

ISBN: 0-515-07608-2

Jove books are published by The Berkley Publishing Group,
200 Madison Avenue, New York, N.Y. 10016.
The words "A JOVE BOOK" and the "J" with sunburst
are trademarks belonging to Jove Publications, Inc.

PRINTED IN THE UNITED STATES OF AMERICA

For Connie

Contents

Introduction

Since the discovery of powerful antipsychotic medications in the 1950s, the mental health field has shifted much of its focus from working with severely disturbed individuals and their problems to the adjustment problems relatively healthy individuals can experience in their daily living. Consider, for example, the impact of the social revolution on morality, the rights of individuals, and the very nature of relationships. For ordinary people the world has become infinitely more complex. Many questions that previously offered themselves to simple solutions have become bewilderingly difficult to answer.

Our parents married, had children and, more often than not, stayed together. Now individuals are uncertain as to whether they want a committed relationship at all, and if so, whether with or without exclusivity. Should it involve simply living with someone? Or marrying that someone? And for how long? Are children to be part of the plan—whether the parents are married or single—and, if a primary relationship is the choice, then, even, what sex will the mate be?

It is neither the "rightness," "wrongness," nor morality of change that is addressed here, but the fact that it exists and that it has an enormous impact on our lives. The world is changing rapidly, and there are too few guideposts or answers to help us mark the way. Normal living has become terribly stressful, uncertain, and anxiety-provoking, and most of us need help in dealing with it. While this is the age of the expert, it is also the age of personal responsibility. And we need to know about ourselves in order to choose a life that is appropriate to our needs. We must also know about, and understand, the world around us so that our choices are realistic and available.

FORMERLY MARRIED describes life from the point of view of a housewife and mother whose marriage has just ended. Marilyn Jensen discusses her feelings of depression, confusion, fear, and excitement about her new status. She shares with us the road to understanding with its myriad twists and turns, ups and downs. We are taken from a state of shock and uncertainty to one of maturity and substance. There is a real sense of *being there* while the first faltering, and then more assured, sense of growth takes place within her.

From mourning to independence and adulthood, the journey is made real to us by the insights and examples from the lives of the author and her friends. There is much of what could be called "enlightened" common sense in this book. It deals with complex issues in a straightforward and sometimes humorous manner that belies its wisdom, but makes it easy for us to understand.

Each chapter has a message of its own. Chapter 8, for example, offers a solution to the ubiquitous problems of parents and their children by redefining the basis of that relationship. The solution, an amalgam of compassion, insight, and practicality, will be appreciated by anyone who has been confused about limit-setting, giving, withholding, and having expectations with regard to others.

It is important to understand that Marilyn Jensen's comments frequently transcend specific issues. While Chapter 8 specifically concerns parents developing a covenant with their children, its comments are applicable to almost all close relationships. While mourning is discussed in Chapters 1 and 2, the insights apply not only to women whose husbands have just left but to all individuals who have experienced the trauma of loss and separation. Similarly, the way back from a sense of emptiness and depression through the development or redevelopment of the self has meaning for us all.

FORMERLY MARRIED acknowledges the common threads that bind us all as we experience and respond to the new and different options in our external and internal worlds. The subtitle, "Learning to Live with Yourself," is most descriptive of what this book offers. You do not have to be "formerly married" to find wisdom here. It is a book that deals with loss, rejection, family, relationships, work, and selfhood. It deals with these issues in a realistic and compassionate manner. It shows us by example that we are more similar than different and that we can abstract from the experiences of others that which is meaningful and helpful for ourselves.

This is an insightful book which dispenses its knowledge in a most comprehensive manner. It does not try to deceive the reader into thinking that life can always be beautiful or that all its problems can be resolved in a few easy lessons. This is not a "how to" book, but a book about *process*. It is about one's ongoing efforts to achieve understanding and, over time, to translate that understanding into action. It is both emphatic and practical. It may not make life all you think it should be, but it will help you move in that direction.

JEROME L. FINE, PH.D.
Clinical Assistant Professor of Psychiatry,
New York University Medical School and
Cornell University Medical College; Faculty,
William Alanson White Psychoanalytic Institute

Preface

This book is a personal sharing of my experience and the experience of others who, formerly married, had to learn how to live with themselves. I have changed the names of those who agreed to share with me in order to protect their privacy.

Each of us walks a singular path. Yet it is reassuring to discover that we often cover the same terrain. Although the view from here is my own, I owe a debt of gratitude to Dr. Jerome Fine, who still helps me see where I have been and where I have yet to go.

Prologue

He was leaving.

The night before, he had packed all his things in the car, so that as soon as the children were told, he could leave. No prolonged good-bys.

We stood at the kitchen door: Billy, a lanky thirteen-year-old, bravely blinking back tears; Ann, eleven, trembling as she clutched my arm; Shawn, nine, her long straw-blond hair falling over her face muffling her tears; I, rigid, my face frozen with fear.

What had brought our family to this moment is not the point of this book. What followed is. For as his car turned the corner out of sight and I turned back into the house alone, I took a first step on what would be a very long journey—learning to live with myself.

• • •

The children ran upstairs and I sat on the edge of the sofa in the living room. Stunned. In my Levi's and T-shirt, with my *Cosmopolitan*s scattered around the room and *The Feminine Mystique* prominent in the bookcase, I might have given the impression of being one of those emerging independent women of the year—1971. Not so. My head was pounding. *Now you can do what you want. I don't know what I want. You don't have to answer to anyone. But then who will question me? You don't need to please anyone! But whom do I please?* I had never had any experience at living alone. All my life up to that moment, every decision I had made, any course I had taken, had always been in reaction, either for or against, someone *else's* idea—my mother's, my father's, my teachers', my husband's—of what *they* thought was best. I'd never seriously considered what *I* wanted to *be;* I only knew what I was supposed to *do:* go to college, work for a while (until I found a husband), and marry and have children, and . . .

So there I sat in the living room of a little suburban house on an early Saturday afternoon. My marriage was ended. I was a thirty-six-year-old mother of three children and I didn't even know what I wanted to be when I grew up.

Maybe life is a series of opening and closing doors. I was thrust onto a new threshold by the slamming of a door behind. And the whack I received, painful as it was, shoved me onto a path I never would have sought for myself.

The end of a marriage is painful. To be suddenly single after a lifetime of dependent relationships—Mom and Dad, roommates, husband—is frightening. But if we can finally accept it as a once-in-a-lifetime opportunity to know ourselves and enjoy ourselves, then it might become possible to find the way to overcome the fear and even rejoice in the years that remain.

I stumbled some. So do we all. Billy, Ann, and Shawn Connell endured my falls, applauded my victories, and grew up alongside me. My new husband, Bruce, walks with me now. This book is dedicated to them. Their love confirms what I have now come to believe. That in learning to live with yourself you can find an abundant and loving life with others.

CHAPTER 1
A Time to Mourn

THE DAY THE MARRIAGE DIES

You have had a death in the family. No, let me put it another way. There's been a death *of* a family—a particular family. And you grieve.

With a death *in* the family there are rituals to perform that can help you overcome grief. Friends come to call. You have arrangements to make, hymns to sing, Scripture to read. There's a funeral.

There is no funeral for the death of a marriage. Yet you grieve. And you need to invent your own rituals to cope with it.

Sitting in the living room of that silent house on the day my marriage died, my only prayer was, *Dear God, let me do something. And let it heal.* I listened for some sound from the children. Nothing. Each of us was paralyzed by our own grief. Then an idea formed in my mind and I almost smiled.

"Bill, Ann, Shawn, come down here!" Slow, ponderous footsteps. Three sad and sullen children appeared on the staircase. They eyed me warily. My words tumbled out.

"Look, I love you. I want to be with you. But we can't just sit here and mope. We have to do something. . . . Let's go somewhere. . . . Let's . . . let's go to the movies!" They stared at me. Then Shawn's eyes lit up.

"The Walt Disney one about the talking duck?" she asked hopefully. Bill and Ann smiled.

"Why not?" I laughed. And as we scurried for our coats and I saw the color coming back into their cheeks, I knew that, bizarre as it seemed, we were doing a healing thing.

We sat together in the darkened movie house for over two hours, chuckling, crying, and occasionally laughing aloud through that silly film. I can't remember the plot. But I'll never forget our closeness: the sudden groping for hands and squeezing so hard my fingers hurt . . . tears on cheeks glistening in the light from the screen . . . whispered I love you's. We touched, we hugged, we laughed and cried all afternoon. When the lights came on and we walked out of the theater into the cool evening air, I felt curiously lighter and stronger. And, I think, so did they.

Going to the movies was our unplanned spontaneous reaction to grief, not a prescription for others, for each person reacts differently. But there *will* be a personal reaction and its value in helping you in your healing process can be measured by two simple questions:

Does it hurt you?

Does it hurt others?

Barbara's neighbors in a small Connecticut town were shocked when she invited a crowd in for a divorce party. "Until we actually went to court, I'd been so involved with the bickering over property, recriminations, the settlement, I hadn't time or energy to consider seriously what life would be like alone. But that day I got home from court, I looked around the house and stared at the emptiness of it, and of my life. I felt as if I'd been raped and thrown into a ditch.

"My marriage had been rotten, but this first confrontation with being totally alone and no one caring if I lived or died, that devastated me. It was sheer terror that drove me to the phone. I called everyone I knew and asked them to come over. Maybe I thought I was having a wake. I don't know for sure. But those who came stayed for most of the night. I fed them. I poured drinks liberally. Eventually we started really laughing and talking and I began to feel better. *Hey,* I thought. *These folks really care about me!* They helped me get through the night. Maybe my neighbors *did* think I shouldn't be partying. But I didn't hurt anybody. What did they want me to do? Crawl into the basement and hide for shame? I tell you this: I knew I needed help and I asked for it. And I got it. That's good, isn't it?"

Yes, it is good. Good to reach out, good to affirm life, good to confirm friendship. Because no one but *you* knows your particular pain. And no one but *you* can prescribe the remedy. This is the moment when you need to treat yourself well. You can indulge yourself, you can do something silly. In fact, it's really O.K. to feel badly, to treat yourself like a sick child, to pamper yourself. As Dr. Lee Salk, psychologist, said in an article on broken relationships in *The New York Times:* "Treat yourself nicely. Indulge yourself in some way—it helps restore self-esteem." And your self-esteem probably needs some restoring.

The end of a marriage, whether it was a good one or a rotten one, raises feelings of self-doubt, questions about your worth as an individual. Dependent people measure themselves by their relationships: When there is none, they have lost their measuring stick. The questions come and you have only yourself to answer. *Why did this happen to me? Could I have prevented it? How can I go on? Where did I go wrong? What's wrong with me?*

There is no graveyard to visit at the death of a marriage—only the graveyard of your own mind that you return to seeking answers, reliving mistakes, regretting lost pleasures, reviving buried pain. No one attends you. No one brings you casseroles. You have to attend to yourself.

It was a full month after the death of her husband that Corrie faced the fact of the death of her marriage.

"Till then, I'd been consumed by *his* death. I'd grieved because of his pain, I'd comforted his family. Friends had mourned with me and left. Then that morning came when I got up and looked around the house and . . . there was nothing I *had* to do. All the thank-you notes had been written. No more visitors would be coming. I was alone. And I would be alone—alone in this house. I had no one to take care of and no one to take care of me. If I weren't a devout coward, that's when I would have killed myself. All I could think was, *I'm a wife. I don't know how to be anything else.*

"I paced back and forth in the living room for God knows how long, and then, there I was in the kitchen on my hands and knees, scrubbing the kitchen floor. For eighteen hours I cleaned the entire house. Every curtain was washed, the fireplace brass was polished. I vacuumed the furniture, straightened the closets, shampooed the rugs. Was I cleaning out my mind? Scrubbing him out of my life? My tears kept splashing into the scrub pail. But you know something? I felt good and useful, doing the thing I could do well. Clean house. And in the doing, I found some confidence. That night —late at night—I fell into my newly made bed, exhausted yet strangely exhilarated. *So there! I can do* something *well*, I thought. It gave me a feeling of security . . . in myself. I knew then that I could get on with the business of living."

Strange behavior? Perhaps, to observers. But I truly believe that it's a perfectly normal reaction to grief. Lacking prescribed rituals, we seek some means of expression, some vehicle through which to dispel pain. To live with yourself is to acknowledge that reaction in yourself, to accept it and permit it to do its work. I call it a conscious therapeutic breakdown. It's freeing yourself from the restraints of what you think someone else is expecting of you, and permitting yourself to have your *own* response to your *own* feelings.

Grief reactions. Do they hurt anyone else? Do they hurt you? If not, let them happen. And be conscious of them. They won't last long, they won't become part of your normal behavior, but they can help you release your pain.

Some reactions *aren't* therapeutic. A drinking binge may ease your pain for a while as it dulls your consciousness. But when the alcoholic haze fades, the pain returns. You've only postponed it, rather than released it. Drugs, murder, and suicide, for obvious reasons, are best avoided. But to scream, to sing, to laugh, to cry, to run, to dance, to work, to sleep—in excess—can be good for you. Let go. And treat yourself well.

MOURNING COMES WITH THE MORNING

He's not coming back. That was my first thought when I opened my eyes the next morning. The other half of the bed was wide and vast as the Sahara . . . a wasteland—a wasted land.

When he and I were married our first purchase had been a standard double mattress and box spring. They sat on a metal frame and served as sofa in the studio apartment that was our first home.

A Victorian brass bed came several years and several homes later. We found it in a junk shop. I polished it lovingly and with pride. We had a real bed! It stood high off the floor. It took climbing into. One did not fall into this bed. One went up *to* bed. There, newborn babies were taken for their early-morning feedings. There, toddlers romped and snuggled to watch Saturday-morning cartoon shows on television. There, too, we made love, argued, and wept. And when our marriage began to deteriorate, it was there that each of us, wordlessly, took our night's sleep on the outer one fourths of the mattress, clinging to the edges lest we fall, or, unwittingly, sprawl in the other direction, cross the chasm in the middle and touch each other.

I bought the twin mahogany pineapple posts at an auction, just a year before we separated. I dismantled the brass bed and put it in the basement, explaining that now perhaps we could get a good night's sleep. The two beds stood respectfully apart, separated by a nightstand.

The day he left he took the brass bed to furnish his new apartment, and I remade the beds, shoving the nightstand into a corner and pushing the two beds together. A king-sized sheet and flowered spread covered it all. It looked like a lover's trysting place. I awoke in it. The expanse of empty bed reminded me: *He's not coming back.*

Beds tell the tale of a marriage.

For those of us who measured our worth by our relationships, the empty bed is an outer, visible sign of our inner failure. What failure? Not a *real* one, but a culturally learned one. It recalls the feelings of not being invited to the birthday party when you were ten years old, not having a date for the sock hop, not getting engaged before graduation. Not "normal."

Gloria is a market researcher with a large corporation in Chicago. She is in the first months of separation from her husband of seven years. At age thirty, she lives alone in a spacious apartment filled with fine American antiques. She is a well-paid executive, bright, attractive, with a sunny disposition that expresses self-confidence and enthusiasm. She travels frequently, goes to parties, dates some. She is involved with her work and appears to have many friends.

See Gloria hailing a cab: golden blond hair tossed impatiently, calfskin briefcase clutched importantly. An enviable picture of a successful single woman.

Then see her as I did, curled into a corner of the sofa in her apartment the evening she agreed to talk with me, and you see another kind of woman: ambivalent, unsure.

"I've been putting up a big front. Really, I feel bitter. I feel bitter because everything I thought my life was going to be in terms of what *I* thought of as *normal* has disintegrated. And in fact my marriage was such a lie that it had to disintegrate. But now . . . I don't exactly know where I fit. Friends are nice and they ask about me, but I don't want to talk yet, I'm not ready to. So I spend a lot of time here, by myself. I guess the fact is, I'm embarrassed. I feel inadequate because I don't have this . . . man . . . this husband . . . this mate. And I wonder what my friends are really thinking.

"All my life I had lived with someone. My family was very close. Then I went to boarding school, college. My first job in New York I had a roommate. For my whole life I had surrounded myself with people. Lived with people.

"Now that pattern is disrupted. It was what I thought my pattern would be, *should* be. And now there is nothing.

"So I put on this happy face and when I see people and they say 'How are things going?' I say, 'Great! Tell me about you!' And they do. Then I come here, and sit. I sit here for hours and think, Oh-oh . . .

"I don't feel this is home at all. I feel like I'm just passing through. And I'm not comfortable with it. Sometimes I think I'm wishing myself as I was at twenty-two, cruising around and having a good time with a lot of other kids. That was my only other experience of being single, which wasn't being alone at all. And I *know* it can't be that way now—my friends are married.

"If you had told me seven years ago that I would be a divorced woman, I would have laughed in your face. Me? Don't be ridiculous! That's insanity."

The four-poster looms in the bedroom, casting a visible shadow through the open bedroom door. Gloria sits in the living room and "thinks."

"I'm an anachronism," she whispers to me conspiratorially as I leave. "Maybe most of us are. We really believed 'it' would last forever."

Anachronisms. The media tell us we're living in the age of "self." But many of us raised in the age of "togetherness" never developed "selves." Like hourglasses we depended on someone else to upend us, if only to keep marking time. Now it's an age of battery-operated digital watches, hourglasses are out of style.

That's how Gloria feels. And Gloria is mourning. Not for her husband really, for she says she doesn't even like him, much less love him. And she's not really mourning for a return to the years of her marriage, for she admits she was living a lie. Yet she mourns. She's mourning the end of dependency, and the loss of security one feels in being "attached" to another. It's the end of belief in an ideal. *I really believed it would last forever.* It hurts.

"I used to be a real busy-bee," she says. "Now I can't even concentrate on television, or read a book. All I do is sit . . . and think . . . and think. I'm angry for the waste of those years. I'm bitter because my life wasn't supposed to be like this. I *know* I'll get over it, but I feel so fragile right now."

•　　•　　•

My mourning period lasted several weeks. During that time I did manage to get through daily chores like laundry and chauffeuring the kids and showing up at the little nursery school where I was a part-time assistant. But I went through the motions like an automaton, avoiding conversations, ignoring the telephone, nursing my pain as one would a sick child.

It would be an overstatement to say that "I took to my bed." But bed was my refuge. There, I would sit up late at night while the children slept, and relive scenes from my marriage, recalling every hurt, remembering little joys, fighting old fights.

I hated sitting alone in the living room. I put the television in my bedroom. Magazines, books, mail, and mending were taken there. I started going to bed earlier and earlier. When I was home in the afternoon and the children were in school, I would go to bed.

Soon I was spending all my free time in bed. And the vast emptiness—that expanse on the other side—became filled. Filled with stacks of books, old letters, magazines, ashtrays, empty cigarette packs, even dried coffee cups. I think it was my unconscious way of trying to withdraw from the reality of my new situation, seeking refuge in the thing that had been a symbol of my security—bed. I filled it with that which was familiar to me and in so doing, filled the emptiness that frightened me.

What was I feeling? I felt *anger.* Lots of anger. I was angry at my former husband for not being who I had thought he was when I married him. I was angry at myself for fooling myself that he was. I was angry at my cowardice that had kept me silent for all those years, when by speaking out we might have found some common ground. I talked to myself. I conducted a dialogue in my head, replaying old tapes of long-forgotten scenes. I hollered. I cried. I punched the pillows. I slept exhausted.

And I felt *embarrassment*. To the world—our friends, neighbors, relatives, even our children—we had played the role of a happily married couple. And now we were found out. Exposed. Scrutinized and talked about. The curious wanted simplistic answers to difficult questions. *How did it happen? Why? What did HE do? What did YOU do? How will you manage?* They were questions I couldn't yet answer for myself. My attempts left me stuttering, tongue-tied, and blushing. So I avoided the neighbors as much as possible, haltingly attempted to explain to relatives, and stumbled through conversations with the children, all the while knowing that what I was saying made no sense.

Later, upstairs in my bed, I would remember those encounters and regret whatever it was that I had said. I felt a fool—an unloving, unloved, stupid old fool.

And I felt *guilt*. The guilt I felt was not the garden variety, "you've done such and such wrong" type of guilt. If it were, I could have made restitution, paid the price, said "I'm sorry," and felt better. No, this was a full-flowering, free-floating guilt—unredemptive. It would catch me unaware as I was about to fall asleep. It would whisper: *You never could do anything right. . . . If only you had tried harder. . . . You never do as you're told. . . . You have failed*.

They were voices from the past confirming my present failure. At those times if I could have worn a scarlet "D" on my bosom I would have done so, or worn sackcloth—anything to quiet those old ghosts.

Nurturing those feelings was a tremendous well of self-pity. I would sit cross-legged on the bed at two in the morning and cry, and cry. Then I would shuffle downstairs to the kitchen and rummage around in the refrigerator for something to eat—*anything* to eat. It might be ice cream or a bowl of cold cereal or even left-over casserole. I would take whatever it was back up to bed with me, turn on the television and watch old movies from the '40s and '50s—*My Little Margie, State Fair*— all the movies that had instructed my young girl's heart about love. I would watch and eat and cry. I would pound my pillow and shake my fist and cry, "Why me?" and shove another spoonful of something into my mouth. Self-pity can be fattening! I was having tantrums. Feeling helpless to cope with the emotional, financial, and social responsibilities of living alone, I reverted to old childhood patterns in a vain attempt to keep adulthood at bay.

I can't say that it was a constructive period of my life. All of that wallowing in my emotions didn't produce a single practical answer to the overriding problem of what to do next. But in a curious sort of way I think now that there was a redeeming quality in my emotional outbursts. For in dredging up all those fears, insecurities, and doubts, I was holding a mirror up to myself that I could finally look into. That I didn't like my reflection was obvious. That I could alter that image remained to be discovered.

CHAPTER 2
When Mourning Ends

In a way, mourning never ends. Sadness strikes at un-
expected moments, triggered by a snapshot discovered
in the bottom of a dresser drawer, a particular phrase in
a mutually loved song, a meeting with old friends. But
the *mourning period,* that time of intense and painful
introspection and self-concern, *can* end if and when you
want it to.

I talked with Ann, a theatrical agent, in the sunny living room of her large sprawling house in Marin County,
overlooking the Bay. Her husband was an attorney.
Ann had always kept up her career through the more
than twenty-five years of their marriage. But at
home . . .

"I was wife, mother, homemaker. Alan was very

good at fixing things, so if something broke in the house, I never had to worry about that. He took care of all the mechanical things . . . and insurance . . . and investments. I took charge of our social life. It was a wonderful supportive relationship and we were so very happy together! And we'd reached that point where we were no longer facing great financial problems as we did when we were younger. Our daughter was almost twenty and on her own. We could travel together . . . enjoy each other's company.''

It was on one of their trips that Alan fell ill. Six months later he was dead and Ann's life unraveled.

"That was the beginning, the first time in my life, of real soul-searching and introspection. I would still go to the office every day, but at night—thank God I had a dog and cat. I'd let myself into the dark house and there they would be, waiting to greet me. It may seem trivial, but it was very important to me that something was alive here.

"Well, then I'd make myself a little supper and take it into the den on a tray and put the television news on. And I would just sit there and think . . . alone. It was the first time in my life that I had lived alone.

"I don't know if we all go through a period of anger when this happens and we say, 'Why me?' But I certainly did. I personalized everything. What had happened to Alan was the *real* tragedy. Yet my first reactions were, 'Oh, my God, how could this happen to *me?*' I'd forgotten that *I* was the one who was still *alive!* No, I was just angry that this could happen to me. I'd done everything right, our marriage was a good one.

"Eventually I started asking myself the question, 'What do I do now?'

"The turning point came when one of the toilets

didn't work, and I found myself in a position where I'd better learn how to do *something* for myself!

"You see, when Alan realized he was failing, he'd said, 'If anything happens to me, you'd better sell the house and move into an apartment because you won't be able to cope with all this.' Well, during that period of introspection I'd remembered those words. They were a challenge! So I taught myself how to fix the toilet—how to take the ball out and replace the ball—I figured it all out. That was a first step. Then I thought that maybe I'd better learn how to do everything for myself because I couldn't be sure there would be anyone else to do it for me.

"How do you learn? Why, the way you learn anything. You read about it. Today, for example, I read an article about weatherstripping that you don't have to tack on. I want to buy some and try it. Look, you don't become a mechanic overnight, but you can learn by figuring out what's wrong and asking questions.

"So I decided I would keep the house. Look, right after Alan's death, I was stunned. I couldn't feel the full implication of all that had happened to me and to him. That came later. There are memories living in the same place. But bit by bit . . . you learn to live.

"It was Christmastime when I think I really turned the corner. Alan had been dead for only three months and Christmas had been a very important time to us. My daughter came home and we decided to have a party— an open house for close friends, people who had been supportive to us. I heard later that some people thought it strange that we should be having a party, but I know now it was the best thing I could have done for myself. It made me feel and experience the continuity of life—to be able to entertain friends. And I was letting them know that I was opening up my life to them. Instead of deciding to be alone, or waiting to be invited, I was inviting them into *my* home and *my* life."

Ann has now been widowed ten years. She is vibrant, busy, loved. She laughs a lot.

"You know, Marilyn," she confided to me, "it's strange. So many of the people who were our friends back then have had a similar experience happen to them. They've lost their husbands, or been divorced. And they come to me and say: 'How did you do it? What's your secret? I'm so unhappy!' But they never invite people into their homes. They don't even invite me. I tell them: 'Open up! Give!' But they're afraid. They're waiting for *someone* to give to *them*.

"It doesn't work that way. You have to seek your own happiness."

How does mourning end? Ann's experience suggests some steps that seem to be essential to your being able to move away from that intense preoccupation with grief.

Acceptance was the first step. At some time during her period of introspection, Ann realized that she had better learn how to take care of herself. That's a reasonable idea for most grown-ups to have, a measuring stick even, that most parents would apply to their own growing children. Yet we who depended on others to take care of us, even though we may have given verbal assent to the value of self-reliance, avoided making an intellectual commitment to it.

Ann did. She sat in her den and took an inventory of her life, saw it as it was, and accepted it. It follows that she then had to learn how to fix a toilet. For an intellectual commitment, not followed by action, becomes meaningless. We all know those who say, "I *know* that I have to take care of myself now, but . . ." Ann accepted it and acted.

Will moved Ann into action. Will is different from the idea of "willpower." That word suggests gritting your teeth and doing something unpleasant that you don't want to do. But *will* is following through with action what you have already determined that you *do* want to do. How do you do it? "You *learn,*" says Ann. You read, you study, you ask questions, you *do.* And in that physical activity, your attention becomes focused on the job at hand rather than on yourself. Bit by bit, says Ann, you *do* learn—and you can enjoy it.

Giving was the step that moved Ann back into the world. She says she opened up her house. But she opened up her heart as well. She gave, not because she owed, not because she expected something back, but because she wanted to share—to give affection, appreciation, and love to others. Ann wasn't keeping score. She didn't wait for someone to give to her before she would give in return. Ann says, "You have to seek your own happiness." Her first steps out of mourning might just be what set some on the right path. For she *is* happy now. Secure and confident.

Of course, each of us has different outer circumstances to our lives. Financial problems can seem overwhelming. Children and close relatives can further complicate our already precarious situation. We all don't live in beautiful houses or have well-paying jobs or the support of friends. But in spite of our circumstances, I think we can learn from Ann. To acknowledge our situation, to accept it; to follow through that acceptance by action; and finally, to focus our attention away from ourselves and onto others; these seem to be healthy steps to take when we're ready to move out of mourning and into the present.

Those who don't move wait. They wait hopefully for someone to rescue them, they wait anxiously for the roof to fall in (or the drain to stop up, or the landlord to put them out), and they wait bitterly for someone to call. They just might wait forever.

And I? Well, it became apparent that I couldn't wait. A broken water main that flooded the street in front of the house and cut off our water supply made me face up to some practical realities and responsibilities. Filling out the application for a loan at the bank, listing my assets (the paid-up portion of the house mortgage and one Volvo station wagon that was included in the divorce settlement), my small teacher's salary; my liabilities (unpaid portion of house mortgage) forced me to look at, in cold black-and-white figures, the financial responsibility I carried and that I had to carry in order to survive. You see, one can't *live* in a house without water. Facing reality was not my choice. It became necessity. Yes, a sympathetic banker approved the loan. And I'm grateful to him to this day, not so much because I got the money for the water main, but because, at that very critical time in my life, he treated me as a responsible person and expected me to live as one. I *would* repay the loan!

Shortly thereafter, catching a glimpse of Shawn sitting midst the rubble on my bed watching a soap opera, the room in semidarkness, the voices of neighborhood children playing outside filtering up through the window, I caught a glimpse of myself.

There, too, I had sat, living "life" vicariously through the images of the television screen and avoiding the real life that clamored outside. I chased her out and she sanguinely went, innocent of the portrait she had created, innocent of the effect of that image on me. And I straightened up the bed, cleaned my room, opened the windows to let fresh air in. Turning the switch on the television, I actually laughed.

Mourning had broken.

CHAPTER 3
Two Steps Forward

So, you've come through a bad time. And you think, *Aha, the worst is over.* You've crawled out of that little self-imposed cocoon. You're trembly, perhaps, like a butterfly with wet wings, ready to fly, solo. You have a lot of decisions to make, and you feel you can begin to tackle them.

You walk through the house. It's home. *Your* home. Should you stay? Move?

Try to look at the house through your eyes only, not the eyes of your former spouse. Why is the furniture arranged as it is? Are the colors to your liking? Do you really want the television in the living room, the ironing board in the basement, the telephone in the study? Was it his study? Will it be yours? Do you even want a study? Heady questions for someone who's not had much practice at answering them, but self-developing ones when you're taking the first steps toward autonomy.

Should you make this place your home? Probably yes. If you can, financially and legally. At least for now.

Ann says: "So many women seem to think that because they've had one big traumatic change thrust upon them they might just as well change everything else in their lives as well. They sell the house, move to an apartment in another neighborhood, get a job (any job), and then can't understand why they are so miserable. They complain about empty lives. They complain that old friends ignore them. But at a very critical moment they moved away from the only possible source of support they might have had.

"Look, it takes a couple of years before you can really get extricated from the emotional toll. It takes a couple of years before you begin to feel like a whole person again.

"And that person will be a different one. You *will* change. But you don't yet know how. So try to let your life continue exactly as it was and let the change come from within. Then you'll be able to make considered decisions as to what you really want to do, where and how you want to live, whom you enjoy being with."

Stay, if you can. I did. At first the house was more museum than home. Certain closet doors remained closed (old clothes he hadn't wanted); five chairs sat around the dining table (the table set for four). I religiously pruned the grapevines he had planted three years earlier that had never yielded grapes, took the car to the same garage (and continued to complain about the poor service), prepared the same meals served at the prescribed hours, stumbled over light cords, banged into furniture.

But gradually, ever so gradually, the house became home. My home. A wing chair that I had bought at a garage sale years ago and that had sat in the basement due to, what? lack of interest? was brought up to the living room. Its new slipcover introduced another color in the room and started an evolution of color—my color—in the house.

One evening, on impulse, I bought myself flowers. For me. A huge spray that I carried home in my arms, my nose buried in the blooms. Hunting through boxes of never-used wedding gifts, I found curious vases and odd pitchers to hold them. Displayed on every available surface in the living room, they might have brought to mind a funeral parlor, but it didn't matter. They were my gift to me—a housewarming gift—and their aroma and riot of color pleased me deeply.

Why do I share these mundanities? Because I truly believe that it's in these simple activities of your day-to-day living that you will begin to discern a subtle change in your spirit. It's the budding of a feeling of pleasure, a growth of self-satisfaction, an enjoyment that comes from caring and being cared for. It's learning to live with yourself.

You don't have to move to the south of France, or to a singles condominium, or to an "over fifties" retirement village in order to create a new life. The materials for that creative act are within and around you. If you use them well, you can create a person who could live reasonably happily *anywhere*.

Lois had to move. Her second marriage, which had

precipitously followed her first, was rapidly disintegrating. His business being located on the property made it imperative that she get out and find a home of her own.

"I had to get away from him, away from the bitterness and disappointment. And, practically speaking, he couldn't move and I could. So I found a little cottage, not too far away, near the people I've always known, took my dog and cat and moved. I was so terribly hurt. I really had thought that this second marriage would cancel out the mistake I made the first time around. I had always grabbed at love (or what I thought was love) and when it happened I drowned in it. I would *be,* and *do,* whatever might please my husband. 'You want purple? I'll be purple. Polka dots? I'll try!' I know now that was stupid, and I have a lot of learning to do about myself, but then—well, I'd never lived by myself, ever, and I had to. So I moved.

"At first it was a relief. A relief to be away from him. Sometimes I'd get a little euphoric. 'God, no one is hurting me today!' And that was enough. But I was floundering. I didn't quite know what to do with myself.

"One night as I was making a little dinner for myself —I'd set the table with candles, linens, the works—I thought: *Hey, this is fun! I really like this.* And it came to me: all the hours that added up to days and years that I had spent in the care and feeding of my husbands. This may sound really terrible, but it was a *thrill* to me that at that particular moment I didn't have to care for and feed somebody!

"I can't get over how much time my husbands *took!* More than a child would take, a very, very young child. Oh, yes, I *gave* it. There's no doubt about that. I was so eager to be wanted, desperate to be needed. But now . . .

"Well, I'm discovering that I can have my own schedule and not wrap my life around another's schedule. I can fix my own elegant dinner, to my liking. I can work late at night on a project with no apologies to anyone. I can call people I know when I want to talk. And time! My time! I've discovered its importance to me. I'm learning what I can do with it. That's how my cottage became my home."

SPACE AND TIME

They belong to you. Space to build your nest; time to manage to your own choosing. All who are heads of their own households have that privilege; those who share a household do not. Even if you have children who sap your energy and demand seemingly impossible time from you, even if your parents or friends or neighbors come bearing gifts of well-meaning advice concerning what they think you ought to do with your time and your space, remember: You are the head of your household. Be it a one-room apartment, a camper, a trailer, or a four-bedroom colonial, it's your household and you can decide for yourself what you are going to do with it and when. You can decide what you are going to do with yourself and when. Hold your head high, you are the head of your household. Rank does indeed have its privilege.

True, you may not have the money to buy the things you'd like for your house, but you don't have to ask anyone *else* for permission to rearrange the furniture, or paint the living room. You may wish that you had more time for your own pleasures, but no one is dictating to you how to manage it. It's *your* conscience that determines whether or not you watch your child's basketball game. It's *your* need that keeps you working at a demanding job and rushing home to clean the house, and collapsing into bed in the early evening. And it's *your* desire that permits you to bake chocolate chip cookies at midnight, write poetry on a rainy Saturday afternoon, or tap-dance the night way.

Every move you make, every breath you take is of your choosing. You may chafe at the responsibility (it's more comfortable to be able to blame someone else for the unhappy state of your affairs—or to earn the approval of another through obedience), but now you have no one to blame and no one to approve. You're on your own!

When Betty was divorced after twenty-seven years of housewifery, at first, she said, she panicked. Although she had been a modestly successful fashion designer for several years prior to the birth of her first child, those long years of trying to make a comfortable home for her husband and subsequent children had distanced her from the world of "making a living" and had conditioned her thoughts and actions to be totally other-centered.

"I felt it was my responsibility to make the people in our family happy. And the easiest way to do that was to ask them what they wanted and try to give it to them. It's incredible, really. I grew up chronologically from being a college kid to an almost senior citizen and apart from deciding that I wanted to get married and have kids I had never asked myself: *What do you want?* I just went along with what everybody else wanted 'cause it was easier.

"Then I was alone. A fiftyish kid in a big house with four nearly grown sons who knew exactly what they wanted and were well on their way to accomplishing it. And they were leaving home to find it.

"Do you know what happened after a couple of months when I was alone? I discovered that I was relaxed! Relaxed in a manner I had never experienced in twenty-seven years of marriage. And, this may seem strange, but it occurred to me that during all those years of marriage I had felt as if I were simply visiting here, and there were obligations to meet or else I would outstay my welcome. I was walking on eggs all the time. Not anymore. This house is home. *My* home.

"And I'm gaining confidence. I think of myself now as a single human being who just might be capable of solving problems, making mistakes, forgiving myself, and trying all over again. And I'm doing it for me.

"An interesting by-product of all this is the tremendous encouragement I get from my children. They seem to see me in a new light now. I think they like me a lot."

Betty is finding her own space, what makes her comfortable. And she's using her time to catch up on some neglected growing.

"I've discovered that every single day that I put off discovering what I enjoy, what pleases me, what I feel is right and good for me, I am trading away another day of my life. And when I bake cookies and take them to my son and his wife, I'm doing it because I really want to, not because I 'ought' to. Isn't that what loving and giving are really all about? The more I develop myself, why, the more I'll have to give away! . . . I need my own time to do that.''

But old habits die hard, and old patterns will repeat themselves if you aren't conscious of what you are doing. I discovered that for several months I was spending the bulk of my free time waiting—waiting for the phone to ring, waiting for the mail to come, waiting for the time to start dinner, waiting for the children to come home, waiting for someone to ask me to do something. Only then would I be propelled into action.

It's an easy trap to fall into. It's comfortable. It's safe. And, you can't be blamed for doing anything wrong, because you haven't done anything at all. And the hours add up to days; the days to years.

A friend confessed to me embarrassedly, ''I'd go to an ant fight if I were asked.'' Well, that's fine if she likes ants. She doesn't. But she is so dependent on others to determine how she spends her time and so fearful of determining that for herself, she'll do anything, if asked. And she waits.

Lois says that the evening she turned down an invitation to dinner with an attractive man she'd been seeing frequently, because she was in the middle of a book she wanted to finish, was when she realized how valuable her time had become to her.

''I said to myself, 'Do you really want to go, or is there something else you want to do?' And of course, there was. And I just told him, 'Not this time.' I know this sounds silly, but I think we have to train ourselves, really train ourselves, to say 'no' when it's in our best interests.

"But I was very nervous doing that because I like him so much and want him to like me. The 'old me' would have just put aside what I was doing—not valued it—and jumped at the chance to please him. Now I put me first. My time, my needs. After all, he's free to do what he wants with his time. So am I.

"I'm not saying this angrily. There's no big confrontation. In fact, none at all, with him. But what fascinates me about this seemingly simple situation is how difficult it was to say 'no.' And how I have to be so alert, watchful, to catch myself from slipping back into the 'old me'!

"I'm just beginning to discover what I can do with my talent and abilities and time. I have to be willing to risk investing in them."

Lois is discovering that her time is valuable . . . as is yours. It's the most valuable asset you hold. Don't squander it.

CHAPTER 4
One Step Back

anx-i-e-ty (ang-ziĕ-ti), n. Painful uneasiness
of mind respecting an impending or anticipated ill.

(Webster)

Anxiety might strike as you're trying to calculate the
price per ounce of the various brands of peanut butter
on the supermarket shelf one late afternoon. Or, driving
alone in the car, the radio blaring, windows rolled up,
air-conditioning humming, you're enjoying a few moments of delicious privacy and it strikes. Or standing in
line at the bank, or riding the bus to work, or walking
down the street on a simple errand, or just before you're
ready to fall asleep, or as you wake. It strikes.

It starts as a tight feeling just below the rib cage. It
rises into your throat, which feels dry and raspy. Your

tongue becomes thick; your breathing shallow. Now
your heart is pounding in your skull. The "thing" is galloping around your head with the speed of a racehorse.

What is it? You're having an anxiety attack. And you
feel afraid. Certainly you're not afraid of the peanut
butter or the groovy music from your car radio. But
what is the reason for this uneasiness which strikes at
odd moments, which reduces you to the state of a
frightened little girl? It's the feeling of going to take an
exam that you know you haven't studied for; of going
to Aunt Minnie's for dinner knowing you spilled your
milk on her pristine white linen tablecloth the last time
you were there; of walking home at dusk past the house
where the big bullies hang out. It's *remembered* fear.
But it feels as real as a reaction to present danger. Yet
you really can't do battle with a jar of peanut butter;
and you're not going to start running away from the line
at the bank, or fight with your car radio. What are you
to do?

NO VALENTINES

Lois explains it this way.

"I've discovered that every time I take a significant
and positive step in my own development, make some
important decision that makes me feel really good about
myself, old 'ghosty' fears seem to surface in my mind
and whisper: 'You can't do that,' 'You will fail,' 'People will laugh at you.' I don't actually hear the words,

but the feelings arise and they can cripple me if I don't deal with them.

"Like last February. There was this three-day weekend that I was really looking forward to. Presidents' Day, Valentine's Day. I was going to get some important writing finished, without any disturbances because most of my friends would be away. I was delighted! You must understand, I wanted this time for myself very much!

"I started working and suddenly I was exhausted. I walked around my room for a bit. I couldn't concentrate on my work, I felt so uneasy. The phone wasn't ringing. I called a few people. No one was home. Of course! It was a three-day weekend and people were gone. I walked down the road to pick up my mail. Nothing. I went back to the mailbox four times. I knew darned well the mailman had been by before my first trip, but I kept going back. I made up reasons to have to walk by the mailbox and open it again, just in case anyone might see me. I was becoming so agitated I could almost feel myself swelling up with nervousness.

"That's when I made myself sit down and say to myself: 'Now, Lois, what on earth is bothering you? You wanted this time for yourself, you love your work, what's going on in you?' I just sat there a while and thought and thought. I went back over what I'd done that day and how I felt. I tried to stand back and observe myself to see if I could find some clue as to what was going on in my head. I looked at my present situation, I considered my past. And then I found it. Of course. It was Valentine's day. I felt unloved.

"Now, I knew that it wasn't me, grown-up Lois, who was feeling unloved. It was that little-girl Lois, who used to feel so wonderful when she got more valentines than any other girl from the big box our second-grade teacher had decorated so beautifully; who was ashamed that her parents were divorced, who had never known her real father, save once, when she had contacted him after her first marriage, met him briefly and then was told he couldn't see her again because *his* wife, *his* children wouldn't understand; who was reminded, over and over again, by her mother, 'Don't let the boys see how bright you are.'

"And there it was, Valentine's Day. I was doing the thing I love—writing. I had planned for it, eagerly, yet I couldn't work because I was full of anxiety. It sounds so dumb, but, you know? I was anxious because I hadn't gotten any valentines!"

The message that Lois was receiving from "those old ghosts" was: *If you succeed at work, you fail at love.* It was a message delivered to her, years and years ago from her mother. Until she could read it, consider its source, and observe its profoundly paralyzing effect on her that day (Valentine's Day!), she couldn't work. Galloping anxiety had her in its grip. Recognizing it, she could do battle with it.

"I called a man I know, a friend who was spending the weekend with his girlfriend and two of his kids who were home from college. I felt shy about calling, you know, butting into someone else's life, but I did and I was surprised. He just said, 'Get here, will you?' So I went. And it was one of the most wonderful times of my life. They were so glad to see me. His kids were playing guitars and we sang. I felt so loved as a person, as *me*, Lois. I needed to have that confirmed right then. And it was.

"The rest of the weekend I worked like a demon! I was so productive, so happy with me. I learned something then that's become very important to me. *I have to figure out what my fears are, how they affect me, and how to alleviate them in a way that's good for me.* Sometimes that means being able to say 'I need,' but with the ability to discern my *real* needs from my imagined ones. You know what I've discovered? There's always some way to meet the *real* ones. It requires asking for help, sometimes, and thinking hard, and figuring things out. But it's the imagined ones that make me anxious. 'Cause in my gut I know I can't do anything about them. I have no control. I'm helpless!'

"I didn't really need valentines that day. And there was no way that I could force them to materialize in my mailbox. What I needed was acceptance. And I had to take the neccesary steps to find it."

STAND BACK AND OBSERVE

At first, I didn't know about anxiety attacks. It took a couple of years for me to see the connection between my sense of aloneness and my hunger for approval from a stern father . . . having no weekend plans and the embarrassment of not having a prom date . . . a mild admonition from my boss and my terror of a scolding from my parents. All no-fault traumas of growing up that most of us have had in one way or another. Until recognized, they live in us as present fears.

I didn't know. But I did know that my hands would shake at odd times; that my telephone bill got so high I was threatened with discontinuance for inability to pay (late-night forays through the phone book seeking a reassuring voice are expensive); that the tight knot in my stomach would ease with just-one-little-drink-to-relax, then another, and another, until I'd fall into a leaden sleep. I knew that I felt afraid, that my feelings didn't logically connect with my day-by-day experiences and that I wasn't coping with those feelings very well.

It was a psychologist-friend who suggested that I simply observe what was happening. "Don't try to get rid of the feeling," he said. "Just observe what happens. How it comes . . . and how it goes. Later you can work on why it comes and how to get rid of it."

It seemed strange advice yet it armed me for the next attack. Driving home after work a week later (a Friday afternoon), it struck. That vague uneasiness in the pit of my stomach. I felt it mount much as I've described it earlier. But this time I would watch it. I pulled off the highway onto a quiet street and stopped the car. With my mind's eye I could "see" the fear rising within me. My hands clutched the steering wheel. *"I am not afraid,"* I kept muttering to myself. "I *feel* afraid." I felt my heart beating, my head pounding. Wave upon wave broke over me. Then it subsided. It was gone. I rested my head on the steering wheel. Whew! I was breathless. But exhilarated. For I'd looked the old demon in the eye and stared it down. And it wasn't as powerful as I had thought. I found out that I could look on it, study it, perhaps in time destroy it.

Anxiety? Sure I had it. But I saw it then as a condition. Like acne. Curable. I could observe it, find out what caused it, control its symptoms and, well, . . . clear it up!

I smiled driving home. And I didn't need something

to relax me when I got there.

Gloria calls them *the dreads*.

"I'd wake up in the morning with this absolutely spooky feeling that something awful was about to happen. I would make myself get out of bed, talking to myself all the while. 'Come on, Gloria. You have to work to eat.' It was only a sheer act of will that would get me into that office with a smile on my face and a big, 'Hello, everybody, how ya doing?'

"Eventually I began to see the dreads as something rooted in my past, a kind of fear of letting other people down. I felt that I'd disappointed my parents, shocked my friends, and hurt my ex-husband. And I dreaded each new day. I feared the responsibility implied in having the power to affect other people. I only wanted to make my parents happy! And I couldn't do that now.

"Just understanding my dread has made it easier for me to handle it. I know where the feelings are coming from. I can observe them, and ponder on them. And they don't inhibit me as they did when I didn't know what they were."

Of course, everyone doesn't get anxiety attacks, but if you do, it's comforting to know that you're not alone. And if you're wondering why—when you've made such giant strides toward getting your house in order; why—just as you've come to a healthy and realistic acceptance of your new role as head of your own household; why—just as you're beginning to taste the sweetness of hard-won independent life—you are suddenly seized with doubts, fear, and despair . . . look into it. You really don't have to live with those feelings. You don't have to be crippled by them. You can understand them, control them, and get rid of them.

CHAPTER 5
Think Shrink

Isn't it odd that the popular term for psychological counseling—shrinking—means "making smaller"? I've never seen any people who have been shrunk by therapy. On the contrary, they seem to stand a little taller. So what is it that gets shrunk? I like to think it's scar tissue (emotional scar tissue from some past experiences) that impedes your present growth. Like adhesions that develop years after surgery, such scar tissue can cause doubling-over pain if not attended to. Yet just as some folk seem to prefer bad health over good, and would rather be crippled with pain than have corrective surgery, so do some seem to prefer to live in a permanent state of unhappiness rather than seek emotional well-being.

My friend Janet told me: "I'd always felt that I was

supposed to handle all my emotional problems, that if I went to a therapist it would be admitting I was crazy or something. I'd say: 'Who needs a therapist? All anyone needs are some really good friends and a big pot of coffee!' Well, I bitched to my friends for years about my unhappy life and they would listen and be very sympathetic. Finally one friend (a *real* one) stared me straight in the eye and said: 'Look, Janet. I can listen, and I can care, but I can't help you. Stick with your misery or get some professional help.' I was shocked, and angry too. But she made me realize that I'd been dumping all my garbage on my friends and they didn't know what to do with it any more than I did. That's when I looked for a therapist. I figured it was time to quit burdening my friends with things they couldn't help me with. Hey, would you ask your friends to perform an appendectomy on the kitchen table, around a pot of coffee? Why expect them to heal your emotional ills?

"No, now that I have my doctor—I call her my *talking doctor*—I'm easier on my friends, and I think I'm more fun to be with.

"You know, I suppose that I could have just lived with my anxieties, compensating for them by not daring too much, or masking them with booze and tranquilizers, and maybe by the time I turned ninety I'd have figured certain things out and not cared about the rest. But, wow! If you have a pain in your gut, you go to a doctor. Why not find one for the pain in your heart?"

Yes, if you have a pain in your heart, do find a doctor —a psychologist, a psychotherapist, a psychiatrist—a *talking* doctor. It's just plain silly for you to have come as far as you have—coping with the end of your marriage, taking charge of your household, managing your time and space—to get shot down by some emotional shrapnel from other old wars. And more changes lie ahead for you. It's nice to have an ally for the battles to come.

WHERE DO YOU FIND YOUR TALKING DOCTOR?

I don't intend to get into a discussion of all the different "schools" of therapy—Freudian, Jungian, etc.—because if you are knowledgeable enough to have a preference for one method over another, you can contact their societies and ask for recommendations. And if you feel totally unsophisticated in this area, there is reassurance in the words of my therapist-friend: "The longer we therapists are in practice, and the more experience we gain, the more our differences diminish." So for now, the only question is: Where do you find your talking doctor?

1. *Word of mouth*. Jane tells Susan that she's "in therapy." When Susan is troubled, she asks Jane for advice. Jane's doctor may not have time for Susan, but will recommend someone whom he respects. It's a haphazard system, but it can work if you assume the additional responsibility of checking the doctor's credentials.

2. *Your medical doctor* (internist, gynecologist, etc.). If your doctor is someone in whom you can confide, you may feel that he or she is the *only* per-

son you can turn to for advice of such a personal nature. But be aware that medical doctors are trained to treat conditions medically—pharmaceutically and surgically. Their particular practice of medicine doesn't necessarily lead them into professional contact with doctors who use an analytic (talking) approach. At best, your medical doctor's recommendation will be confirmed by your own queries elsewhere. At worst, you could be directed to someone who will treat you medically, masking your condition with drugs—uppers, downers, and levelers.

3. *Your spiritual leader*. Pastors, priests, ministers, and rabbis would seem to be natural resources. They may counsel you themselves or recommend a trained therapist for more intensive work. Remember that they do hold certain theological beliefs that predispose them to lead you toward those beliefs, and to recommend someone who supports them.

4. *The Mental Health Association*. Professional therapists are registered with the association. Maybe you have a mental health clinic in your town, or on a county-wide level. Ask for referrals.

5. *University hospitals*. Inquire at the psychiatric division. It will quite likely have a referral service that can put you in touch with therapists who once studied there or are presently working in the department.

INTERVIEW

Don't feel intimidated! Remember that it is *you* who are taking this journey. You have every right to demand a good guide and traveling companion. Apart from feeling that you can be comfortable with your talking doctor, the two very important criteria to look for are *training* and *experience*. A therapist's professionally recognized training in an analytic method of therapy and a history of successfully treating people such as yourself are the safeguards that you'll want to look for before you make a commitment.

You may interview several therapists before you find someone you feel really comfortable with. That's O.K. But as one pointed out to me, "If you see fifteen and still aren't comfortable with anyone, maybe that's part of your problem."

Everyone isn't in need of some kind of long-term therapy. Sometimes a few visits with a talking doctor can help clarify a situation and dispel groundless fears. Just don't be afraid to look for help. Use that search as one more experience in learning to take responsibility for yourself and your own long-term well-being.

The "dark night of the soul" can be just that—one dark night. It need not grow to fill a dark lifetime. Depression, anxiety, low self-esteem, and any other troubling condition that keeps you from tasting the sweet joy of being alive are only conditions. They *can* be healed.

Some wonderful adventures lie ahead, as well as real tests of strength and endurance. Meet them in good health.

CHAPTER 6
Single on Noah's Ark

You'll notice it:

When you don't receive an invitation to Bob and Alice's annual Christmas party . . .

When in spite of notifying everyone of the change in your marital status, you continue to get announcements of the Couples Club's progressive dinners . . .

When certain married women friends only invite you for lunch rather than the occasional evening drop-ins you and your husband used to enjoy with them and their husbands . . .

When other husbands who used to engage you in conversation or frivolous repartee seem distant and slightly nervous in your company . . .

• • •

You'll notice it.
You're single on Noah's ark.

Not more than a month after my husband and I
separated, I got a phone call from Lynn. She and her
husband had shared many an evening with us. I considered her a friend.

SCENE: *Kitchen. Pile of dirty laundry on floor.*
Clothes washer and dryer making customary
noises. Marilyn, folding clean bath towels, is
humming to herself. She appears happy. Tele-
phone rings.
MARILYN: Hello?
LYNN: Well, hi there! Seems like I can never get
    you at home anymore. How ya doin'?
MARILYN: Oh, pretty good. It's been quite a
    time, you know.
LYNN: It's been so long since I've seen you. I've
    really missed you.
MARILYN *(warming):* I've missed you too.
LYNN: Well, that's what I'm calling about. John
    and I are having some friends in for dinner next
    Saturday. Will you be able to come?
MARILYN: Why, how very nice. I'd love to!
    (Thinking kind thoughts about the constancy of
    friends, etc.)
LYNN: We'll see you both, then?
MARILYN: Well, uh . . . I guess you haven't
    heard. . . . We . . . uh . . . separated. Last month.
(Long stretch of silence)
LYNN: Oh.
MARILYN: But I'm fine . . . and gee, thanks for
    the invitation. I'd like to see you.

LYNN: W-e-l-l. Maybe some other time. O.K.?
MARILYN: Right. Bye. (Marilyn *returns phone to cradle, slowly.*) Well. So it goes.

It was the first time I'd ever been *dis*invited to a party! And it hurt. It hurt very much. I was angry, too. And the anger lasted for several weeks. But as I came to understand the implications of being single on Noah's ark, the anger faded, the hurt subsided, and indifference filled that space. Not indifference toward life, but indifference toward people like Lynn. For I saw that we'd *not* been *friends*—only two halves of two couples who'd been riding the ark together.

THE OTHER HALF

It's difficult to perceive of *Mrs.* John Jones as an individual. And if John Jones is the banker or plumber or teacher or fireman or engineer or corporate executive in your neighborhood (in other words, if *he* has a clearly defined role), who is *she?* When Mr. and Mrs. Tom Johnson have a dinner party, they invite Mr. and Mrs. Bruce Healy, Mr. and Mrs. Murray Adams, Mr. and Mrs. Jack Mason, and, of course, Mr. and Mrs. John Jones. And each invites the others in turn.

This pattern of social intercourse goes on in every village, every city, every neighborhood in the country. Certainly it's not the only pattern—there are arts and letters groups, sports enthusiasts, political cells—but chances are if you've been married for a good number of years and lived in one community over a period of time, you and your husband were a part of that pattern. And if your work was secondary to his and primarily supportive of him and his work, then your value to the pattern was as his *Missus*. You were the other half of a couple.

So, what happens to Mrs. John Jones when Mr. John Jones splits, or dies, or moves away? To those who are committed to the couples pattern, she simply ceases to exist. Like producers of a stage play, they'll call Central Casting for another couple to fill the space so the show can go on.

Does it really matter? Of course not! You, your personality, your gifts, your individuality, are of far more value than to be accepted or rejected on that basis. But the first shock of recognition stings. And if you believed these people would be your friends, if you thought your social life could continue in much the same pattern as before, if you felt that *Shirley* Jones could maintain the same social position as *Mrs. John* Jones, you just might be a little disappointed.

Don't let it get you down. Don't blame yourself. And don't try to regain your position with them. You will develop new patterns for living that will be far more fulfilling than that old pattern. Friends have more fun!

THAT MERRY-WIDOW/GAY-DIVORCÉE TRAP

Everyone has at least one tale to tell.

The doleful pillar of the community who mourned Corrie's husband's passing with lengthy oratory and copious tears, then, meeting her on the street one morning as she walked to work, offered additional consolation and financial support, too, since she "must be having a terrible time adjusting to life without a man." And his wife would never know.

The suddenly skittish wife of a man I'd been having political arguments with for years, halting my heated rebuttal in mid-sentence by grabbing his arm and dragging him across the room, insisting he had to try the cheese dip *now*.

The prurient prying by Toni's boss:

"He's always been very supportive of me and my work and kept a respectable distance—very professional and businesslike. But when I was divorced he started asking me those odd questions at our Monday-morning meetings: 'How's your love life going?' . . . 'I'll bet you had a really wild weekend.' . . . 'How do you young women cope with all this sexual liberation?'

"At first I thought he was just being concerned and fatherly. It was a real effort for me to answer his questions. I felt so uncomfortable. I'd never asked him about *his* sex life. But he was my boss! And the truth was I had no love life at all at that time. My weekends must have seemed pretty dull. I did laundry, wrote letters, cleaned my apartment, and sometimes went to a movie with a girlfriend. So, I'd tell him that. He hated it!

"One morning he glared at me and said: 'A pretty girl

like you ought to have lots of dates. What's the matter with you? Don't you like *real men?*'

"I was speechless. What did he want me to tell him? I'd been earnestly trying to reply to his questioning as honestly as I could. But he didn't like my answers. It took me a while to sort it out, but I finally came to understand that this conservative, comfortably married man with four children actually *expected* me to be bouncing around from bed to bed with young lovers! And if I wasn't doing that, and I hadn't made a pass at him, well, was I somehow not normal? a man-hater? a lesbian?

"Gee, I was really depressed. I liked my job and honestly liked him too. He was solid, reliable, good to his wife and kids. I wanted to keep working with him. I *needed* that job. There was just this one problem . . . with me.

"I started lying. Just a little. Enough to satisfy his curiosity and to assure him that I was, indeed, a healthy 'normal' woman who wouldn't cause him any problems —personally or professionally. When he'd say, 'How was your weekend?' I'd beam, then smile shyly and whisper, 'Fantastic!' with a look that said, 'We'd both be embarrassed if I told you.' He'd shake his head knowingly and ask no more. And then I'd let drop little references to my 'friend' with whom I was going out to dinner, spending weekends on the beach, catching the latest shows.

"He stopped asking questions and we got back to a business-as-usual relationship. Weird as it may seem, I think that by my feeding his fantasy of a 'normal healthy woman,' he was able to relax, knowing that I wouldn't make him uncomfortable personally. I was safely *attached.*'

• • •

Formerly married women *do* arouse curiosity and suspicion in the minds of some married folks. *What does she do for companionship? How does she get along without sex? Is she going to make a play for me? Is she after MY man? What's she got against men, anyway?*

The merry-widow/gay-divorcée myth is still at work in the subconscious minds of many, many people who, try as they may to deny it, feel threatened by the very presence of an unattached female. And the less secure they feel in their own marriages, the more persistent is the lure of the myth. For as they daydream what *they* would do if only they were "free"—as they imagine their spouse's funeral, a secret affair, a younger partner—the myth fuels their fantasies and directs their dreams.

That you are feeling neither gay nor merry is beside the point. You are a walking, living, breathing dream. You'll be observed, scrutinized, applauded, and scorned to the extent that you ease their fears and fulfill their fantasies.

Sounds silly? I know it's not when my friend Mary tells me of going to her office Christmas party unescorted and seeing the men with whom she shared daily comradeship suddenly freeze.

"They'd all brought their wives. And the office women had brought their husbands. I was the only one unattached. The men wouldn't laugh and joke with me as they usually did in the office. I guess they were nervous about what their wives would think. And the women eyed me warily and stuck with their husbands.

"I was so embarrassed. No one had said, *with escort only,* and, besides, I wasn't dating at all, at that time. I couldn't have *paid* anyone to escort me!

"They sat me at a table and we all talked . . . politics, business, house repairs. They were really very kind and attentive. But over in the corner a little combo was playing and no one would go onto the dance floor. You see, they were too polite to leave me alone; too uneasy to ask me to dance. So the band played on and we talked on—until, mercifully, the party was over.

"I'd only gone to the party as a business obligation. Had I known I'd make everyone so uncomfortable, I wouldn't have gone at all. I felt badly about that."

Mary, a divorced, middle-aged businesswoman, was raising three teenagers and running an eight-room house singlehandedly. She was exhausted much of the time. That she would be a sexual threat to someone else's wife, in *or* out of the office, was the furthest thing from her mind, desire, or inclination. But old myths die hard. Even if your face looks like a road map of worry lines and your hips are beginning to look like saddlebags; even though you haven't bought a new slip in four years and your shoes are getting run down at the heels; even when you go out of your way to keep your distance from attached men and protest any suggestions to the contrary, the myth persists. Unaware, you can find yourself cast in the leading role.

Because you are . . . well, let's face it.

Available.

THE HELPLESS WOMAN

Some couples are very kind. Perhaps *too* kind for your own good. In the first flush of their concern for you as a newly single woman, they call, they invite you to little dinners, they take you to the movies. When the drain gets stopped up in the kitchen, he comes over with his tool kit and spends his Saturday morning getting it unstopped. She offers to baby-sit the kids if you have a date. When they're having a party, they make sure you're included. One of them always picks you up and returns you home when the party's over. They are simply wonderful.

We all want friends like these. And especially after a long siege of grief and mourning, caring friends do much to help you get back into the mainstream of living, providing just the right kind of personal attention that makes you feel loved and lovable.

But if after a few months—or a few years—the calls are less frequent and the parties fewer, consider. You may be victim of the helpless-woman convention. What was once their pleasure has become their burden. Even though you are perfectly capable of getting to and from their home unescorted, know how to call a plumber and hire a babysitter, and want to pay your own way to the theater, they don't/won't believe you. You are a woman. Ergo, helpless.

If you've allowed yourself to accept their special treatment of you, and have come to expect it, watch out. You're setting yourself up for a falling off—the gradual deterioration of a friendship into an occasional get-together when they have the time, money, energy, and inclination to take care of you.

The helpless-woman convention operates in the minds

of many without any assistance from you. After all, *she* wouldn't know how to take care of a stopped drain; *he* wouldn't want *his* wife to travel alone at night; he *always* picks up the tab when they go out. It's very sweet, really, that they feel compelled to treat you specially. But it's also a drain on their time and their wallets. They can't *afford* to see you! If their conventional thinking precludes their acceptance of your willingness to carry your own weight and pay your own way, well, they may, of necessity, see less of you.

Even with my friends Marion and Ladd—a couple whose home was an "anytime drop-in place" where we could argue politics until two in the morning, cry over a late-morning pot of coffee, laugh at the antics of our growing kids—we got caught temporarily in the convention.

A spur-of-the-moment decision to go to the movies and grab something to eat afterward would result in Ladd's shelling out the fare for the three of us. It felt natural for me to defer to Ladd; it felt comfortable for him to "take care of the check." I would dutifully offer to pay. He would graciously demur. That's what a man is supposed to do, right?

"Wrong," I told Ladd one tearful evening as I stuffed some bills into Marion's handbag. I'd been observing a foursome at the next table settling the check, both men contributing equally to pay the bill. "Why should it cost you more to go out with me than with just another couple?"

We realized then that we had to break with the convention of taking care of "the helpless woman." For, in truth, I was not helpless. I represented one household, they another. We had to honor that fact if our friendship were to thrive. We did. And it did.

It's good to remember that you *are* the head of a household when you're tempted to play into the helpless-woman convention. For along with the freedom to control your own space and manage your own time goes the responsibility of taking care of your own self. Sure, it's right to accept gifts freely offered and favors proffered. And it's wonderful to have the kind of relationship with friends that permits asking for help. But if you act helpless when you're not and if you take all favors as your "due," then you're feeding the helpless-woman convention and abusing the friendship.

Some friends will doggedly cling to the convention for their own psychological reasons. He feels more masculine; she confirms her dependency. Their perception of your helplessness makes *their* marriage feel more secure. There isn't much that you can do about that, other than not being terribly surprised and hurt if they don't include you in their plans as often as they used to.

Unless they're willing and able to change their perceptions of you . . . well, that's just the way they are.

MAKING PEACE

Oh wad some power the giftie gie us
To see oursels as others see us!
It wad frae monie a blunder free us,
    An' foolish notion.

Robert Burns

● ● ●

To be seen, and accepted, as we see ourselves is an aspect of grace—that transcendental experience of knowing and being known, reserved for the deepest spiritual experiences of God and reflected in rare intimate human encounters. To expect that kind of "seeing" of all relationships is, at the very least, wishful thinking; worse, arrogant.

You can, of course, choose to scorn the insecure, the anxious, the dependent, the frail—all whose perceptions are clouded by remembered fears, all who carry around some emotional baggage from other experiences, all who sought or are still seeking security in the structure of socially defined roles—and your world will get very small.

The ark is loaded with all kinds of creatures wearing many different glasses through which they view you and everyone else. It takes time and courage to choose a new prescription—just as it has taken time and courage for you to alter your view of yourself and others. Have compassion. Forgive them.

I say this, for I have known so many widowed and divorced women who have harbored deep resentment toward couples who "dropped" them, men who made passes at them, women who mistrusted them—such bitterness that they simply jumped ship, angry over misunderstandings, hurt because love seemed to be passing them by. The wounds they have inflicted on themselves by their isolation are far more damaging than any retaliatory attempts at evening the score. For love *does* pass them by. The ark sails on without them.

Forgiving yourself is important, too, if you are to make peace with others. As you become more comfortable living with yourself, as you become more independent in your decision-making, as you gain confidence in your own abilities, you'll find some of your values changing. You may reconsider how you want to spend your time and with whom. Old pleasures may grow stale; old friends may bore.

Feeling guilty for this disaffection can only lead to trying to place blame—on yourself or on the other—for the natural ebb and flow of honest human relationships that grow under certain conditions and fade under others. That others may attempt to blame you for the fading away of a relationship is really *their* problem; if you assume the blame, it becomes *your* problem.

Forgive. Two thousand years ago a Galilean gave a five-word blueprint for successful human relations. "Love your neighbor as yourself." To love is to forgive. And the breadth of your love for your neighbors can only extend as far as the depth of your love for yourself.

Stay on the ark. Stay involved in the world, however flawed. You'll have joys and disappointments. Lose some old friends and gain some new ones. And in the work of staying afloat, you just might discover some hidden riches within yourself and others. Maybe not a pot of gold at the end of a rainbow, but definitely a rainbow.

CHAPTER 7
Staying Afloat

So you aren't moving to a singles condo, you aren't into an affair with your lawyer, your doctor, or your former husband's best friend, you're not going home to Mother, you're not moving in with the children—in other words, you're staying put. If the structure of your life is going to remain pretty much the same (sans mate), you'll want to figure out how to stay afloat on that ark.

Yes. You will be perceived differently by some. But you can handle that if you remember that it's *their* problem, not yours. You only really want the friendship of those who are able to appreciate you as an individual, don't you? Those who won't—or can't—aren't important.

Take a tip from Ann:

"Sure, there were a few people who dropped me.

After Alan died I never heard from them again. Later, when I'd run into them at the market, or wherever, they'd say, 'Oh, we must get together sometime.' Well, *pfft!* Who needs that? There are too many good people around to waste your emotions on others!''

Where do you find the good people? One way, says Ann, is through your work. If you have a job, look upon your business associates as a foundation for a whole network of friends.

"I know so many widows and divorcées who have thrown themselves wholeheartedly into their work, yet never consider that the people they worked with could be a foundation for a social life. They work long, hard hours, then go home and close the door behind them. They dream of going on a cruise or taking an exotic vacation to make their lives rich and full again. Believe me, the potential for richness is right next door, in the next office, across the street, around the corner.''

Ann has built a social network of neighbors and business friends that satisfies her desire for intellectual stimulation, variety, and congeniality.

"But you have to be willing to give to them without expecting something back—other than your own enjoyment in the giving. You introduce them to each other. You delight in their discovery of each other. And then you meet *more* people through those whom you already know. Open your doors and ask them into your life!''

Yes, as Ann insists, with some experimentation, a measure of assertiveness, and a dollop of generosity, you can create an active social life that satisfies you. Because you are widowed or divorced does not mean that you have to go to Club Med and Parents Without Partners and singles bars to find companions. You need not be condemned to a world of bridge luncheons and nights alone with the television.

I joined the local theater group. It had long been an interest of mine. I had even done some professional acting in earlier years. The theater seemed to be a natural place for me to put my energies. I cared about the quality of the productions and I enjoyed the work.

Caring and enjoyment are two qualities you'll need to bring to any civic group you're thinking of joining. *Don't* join a group for the sole purpose of meeting people. The group will be looking for your commitment. If you have it you'll be appreciated. If not, they'll dismiss you.

I emphasize this because I'm sure that you, as I, have probably heard the advice of counselors to lonely widows and divorcées: *Join a club! Meet people! Make friends!* Little is said about *what* club, *why*, and how you can participate. Before you join up, assess yourself. *What are you interested in? What do you want to learn? How much time and effort do you want to give? How much do you care? What do you enjoy?* Be honest with yourself.

I remember that each fall, when our theater's season would begin, a fresh group of lonely folks would wander in to volunteer. That they were single, widowed, divorced, rich, poor, ugly, or attractive wasn't really our concern. If they shared in the group's goals and were willing to give their time, energy, and hearts to help achieve them, they were embraced. Those who were only concerned about themselves and shied away from taking any responsibility would hang around for a few weeks and eventually wander out, as lonely as when they first appeared.

Sad? Yes. But, I think, realistic. Whether it's a political party or an arts group or an education lobby or the Clean Air Committee or a taxpayers revolt, you'll be just as lonely in the crowd as at home watching television if you don't care about the group's goals. *Your* efforts should give *you* satisfaction. The work is your reward. And the nicest surprise is that you'll then discover that friendships do evolve—not from your seeking them but as a natural by-product of a shared commitment.

No, don't join a club to meet people. Discover your interests and make a commitment to them. Then you *will* meet people. People who will be delighted to meet you.

. Some of my happiest memories are connected with that theater: building sets on a cold Saturday morning in November as the wind whistled through the unheated auditorium, trying to hammer and saw, wearing mufflers and mittens, laughing at our ludicrousness, warmed by our camaraderie; clutching the stage manager's hand tightly while waiting in the wings for her to give me my cue to go on stage, nearly smothering in her bear-hug embrace when I returned on the wave of the audience's laughter at my (at last!) well-timed line; sitting in the last row of the darkened house, giggling with another cast member at her husband's antics, gasping as he smashed into furniture, cheering at his improvising genius at stopping a show; late-night coffee klatches, family picnics, weddings, funerals, christenings—the theater people were all members of the same family, held together by a common goal. Yes, there were squabbles and rivalries, just as in other families. And yes, some members were standoffish, performing their tasks in a singular fashion, taking their pleasure solely from the work itself. But all shared in the joy of accomplishment and respected each other's contribution to it.

That's how it is with clubs—people with a common interest. Discover your interests, invest in them and make a commitment of time and energy to them. Friends will follow.

And how about your church or synagogue? Do you shy away from following your inner spiritual leanings because your congregation is so family-oriented? Or because it seems to be a gathering of pious widows? Or because only old people go to church?

Heeding social perceptions and following them at the expense of your faith can be a dry and lonely route.

Betty and her family had been fairly active in their church. It was the axis of their social life, for the boys as well as for her and her husband. Divorce after twenty-seven years of marriage made Betty feel separated from the church, left out.

"I struggled with feelings of guilt, embarrassment, and failure. I imagined everyone condemning me, and, quite frankly, I was nervous about their acceptance of me. Now, I know that all those feelings were *social,* they had nothing to do with religion or things spiritual. But those were my fears. After all, church had been a social thing for our family. I'd accepted the spiritual part as simply an adjunct to it.

"It was during the time when the divorce was being finalized and I couldn't sleep for worry about how on earth I would be able to support myself that those words from Matthew in the New Testament came to me: 'Consider the lilies of the field . . . ,' and I recalled the promise that surely God would take care of me as well as He has His creation.

"It may seem odd to anyone who doesn't believe in a

caring Creator, but the recollection of those words gave me a feeling of security, of being taken care of, that I hadn't felt before. My faith in God grew stronger as I did.

"I started going to church alone. Not for social reasons, nor for community acceptability, but because I wanted to worship. I wanted to grow in my faith and strengthen it through the practice of it."

Betty became a deacon in her church and actually met a widower there whom she eventually married. Of course, she may not have. She wasn't going to church to meet people or to find a husband. She was listening to her inner voice and following it. And perhaps that's the real secret of staying afloat in your community: listening to your inner voice, having the courage to heed it and the confidence to follow it. Fellowship and friendship with like-minded people naturally follow.

And you can do things alone. You don't have to have a companion to see a movie or go to a concert.

"Why," says Gloria, "is going to the movies alone such a big deal for us women? Why are we so hung up about having to have a *date?* How many experiences have I missed because I had no one to accompany me?

"*The Tin Drum* was playing at the theater near my apartment, and I'd been trying to find someone to go with me. Finally I knew if I didn't go by myself, I'd never see it. It's crazy, but I thought about it all day long at the office. And I thought, *Gee, here's another thing I'll miss out on,* and I said to myself, 'O.K., kiddo, you're going!'

"Isn't it funny that I, big-business executive—smart, with-it young lady—would feel so . . . so vulnerable and scared standing in line at the theater? I can laugh now, but then I had these weird thoughts like . . . people were *noticing* that I was alone . . . like I was some kind of social pariah.

"Well, I picked a seat in an empty row. Wouldn't you know? A gang of couples sat right behind me. And they wouldn't stop talking. Finally I turned around and said to them very sternly, 'For heaven's sake, shut up!' They did, and I settled down in my seat. I hunched my knees up to my chin and gave all my attention to the screen. Then I had to smile. You know, I was actually *happy* to be seeing this film alone. No one would distract me. I could enjoy it—all by myself.

"What a wonderful discovery for me! There are certain experiences I particularly *relish* alone. I don't need a companion, I don't have to wait for a date to take me. I can take myself and enjoy my own company.

"I'll always remember *The Tin Drum* because it was a fabulous movie—a moving and horrific and totally absorbing tale—but also because it marks a little step on my journey of learning how to get some richness out of living when you're living alone. You've got to take it for yourself and not sit around and wait for others to give to you."

Alone or with others, you can "get some richness out of living." You may feel a little strange, at first, going out alone. You may feel slightly self-conscious when you go to a party unescorted or on your first foray into public life, community organizations, social groups. But as Betty, Ann, and Gloria confirm, you can follow your interests alone and enjoy them. Or you can choose to be bored; choose to be lonely; choose to wait. It's *your* choice.

A FEW REMINDERS FOR GETTING ALONG

Now. With all your resolve, burgeoning interests, burning commitments, and generous spirit you're ready to throw yourself into the arms of those on the ark. Don't forget that the traps are still there. You're still the single person in a "coupled" community. With that in mind I offer a few suggestions gleaned from my own experience and from others that might serve to make for smoother sailing.

1. *Don't flirt with your host.* If he invites you out into the garden to see his tomato plants, or up to the third-floor bedroom to admire his new wallpapering job, don't go alone. A few drinks may have momentarily raised his fantasy level, but he'll have forgotten your refusal by morning. His wife, however, will not forget your acceptance. She makes up the guest lists.

2. *Don't acknowledge a pass.* When someone else's husband says, "We really ought to meet for lunch someday," or "Gee, I get lonely when my wife's visiting her mother," play dumb. If he meant nothing by it, you've spared both of you embarrassment. If he did mean something by it, remember that acknowledgment demands an answer. And hell hath no greater fury than a man rejected.

3. *Don't talk about your former husband.* Sure, you'll want a confidante. That's a private relationship. But don't bore your friends with more than

they ever wanted to know about him just because they weren't afraid to ask, "How are you getting along?" Give a polite question its due: a polite answer.

4. *Don't act like a pickup*. Presumably you're where you are because you want to be there—not as a prelude to something or someone better. Find something interesting about the ninety-year-old lady on your right, the stockbroker on your left. The stranger across the crowded room will find you, believe me.

5. *Don't feel hurt*. Many people are thoughtless, some dumb, few cruel. It's *your* decision to spend time with them. If they behave boobishly, you can forgive them. If they treat you shabbily, you can walk away. But they really can't hurt you. Hurt is something you do to yourself when you *expect* more than is offered. Observe people. Accept them as they are . . . or don't. Know that it's your choice, not theirs.

6. *Do find a way to pay your own way*. If his ego won't allow it, slip it to his wife with the explanation, "You'll understand, I know," or privately speak to the waiter and arrange to prepay the check, explaining, "It's *my* turn." They'll be surprised at first, maybe even offended—but privately pleased.

7. *Do handle your own transportation*. If you don't own a car and live miles away from public trans-

portation, you'll obviously have to ask for help. Otherwise, there's no reason why you can't get around on your own initiative. Arriving alone is a strong, healthy statement of your independence; a well-planned departure allows for gracious farewells and relieves your host of the onerous task of finding someone to take the "poor woman" home.

8. *Do raise your interest rate.* Investing in your own interests, your own pleasures, can yield great returns. Are you concerned about the quality of education in your community? Go to the school board meetings. Do you like music? Go to concerts. Want to learn more about theater? Join the amateur theater group. Go to the movies you want to see, the community meetings you care about, the courses you'd like to learn more about. And don't be afraid to go alone. If you're truly interested, if you honestly care, you'll be welcomed. It's your commitment that counts, not your marital status.

9. *Do entertain yourself.* Don't wait to be entertained. Do you like parties? Have one. Are there people you'd like to see? Invite them. Social intercourse doesn't have to be a tit-for-tat arrangement. Give without expecting to get. You're doing it for your own enjoyment and that's reward enough.

10. *Do value your self . . . above all else.* Your self is a most precious gift for your children, your neighbors, friends. Treat your self well. Respect it. You'll find you like keeping company with you, and like keeping company with others who do. The rest don't matter.

• • •

If the above do's and don'ts seem obvious or terribly simplistic to you, I bring them to your attention only because each was arrived at through some consciousness-raising experience of mine: the dinner party where I earnestly tried to explain my divorce, jabbering away as the guests' eyes glazed over—the roast getting cold, the ice cream melting; assuring a hostess that I honestly *was* admiring the vegetable garden of her elderly, fatherlike husband—mud on my shoes, brambles in my hair; belatedly discovering that a party was over, the others had departed, and no one had offered to take me home.

Minor gaffes. Small embarrassments. But they made me aware of my new responsibilities to others and for myself, that innocence is no excuse for hurt feelings and misunderstandings.

And there were tiny triumphs that gave me courage to try, to explore new ways of getting along; discussing a play I had seen alone, giving my singular opinion, "I feel . . . ; I think . . ."; the delicious afterglow of a gathering of thirty disparate people, carefully selected for my own enjoyment, each reflecting their pleasure at mine; the shared pride of accomplishment with the amateur cast and crew of *The Fantasticks*, knowing each of us was necessary and important; feeling the warm embraces of couples like Marion and Ladd who expected more of me than I did and loved me into loving myself.

To this day I can still relish the memory of those first-time experiences on my journey to learning to live with my self and enjoying it. Perhaps to a *non*dependent woman they seem ordinary, even adolescent. But I think that for dependent women who are struggling to grow up and live comfortably in their communities it's helpful to know that their struggles aren't singular ones. And that finding the way to make peace with your fellow passengers, then pulling your own oar, is a reasonable way to manage to stay afloat.

CHAPTER 8
What's Going to Happen to the Children?

"Mommy, do I have to tell people?" (Shawn on her way to school)

"Oh, my dad's just away on a business trip." (Ann to a young visitor)

"I used to look down on kids who came from broken homes. That's me now." (Billy at bedtime)

I had expected them to feel badly, to be concerned. I hadn't anticipated their personal embarrassment and loss of self-esteem. Don't think that kids are more sophisticated these days and that divorce doesn't bother them very much. It does. And when a father dies:

"She should have kept him alive. That's all I could think. And she was feeling so sorry for herself. I felt like an orphan."

75

"Even though my daughter's married, she still seems to be searching for that man, the father, that she lost."

"Dad's dying killed my dream for the future. I've been angry for ten years. I'm finally getting over it now."

Survivors of the death of a marriage feel betrayed. A promise has been broken. After all, no parents warn their children that they may be gone tomorrow. And children *do* believe their parents: "Don't worry, Daddy's right here." . . . "Don't cry, I'll be right back." . . . "Silly. Mommy and Daddy will never leave you." Those are reassurances that we parents gave our children to foster in them a sense of security and to build bonds of family trust.

Death and divorce break that trust. A child has been betrayed. Dare your child trust you again? What will your next promise be?

The courts may call it guardianship or custody—neat legal terms that define where your child's hat will hang —but parenting doesn't occupy a clause in the contract. You have to write that one yourself.

A COVENANT WITH YOUR CHILDREN

I like the word *covenant*. It goes beyond contractual agreements and tit-for-tat arrangements of "if you do thus and so for me, I'll do thus and so for you." Covenant suggests that security and warmth of those Old Testament words God spoke to the Children of Israel when they pulled up stakes, fled Egypt, and began a forty-year wandering in the wilderness: "You will be my people and I will never let you go."

Covenant doesn't barter for favors, or even love, in return. It isn't earned. It can't be bought or sold. It's unconditional.

It took me several years to understand the importance of covenant in my relationship with my children. There were times I felt like a martyr, questioning, *Why me?* When money was tight and I had to forgo buying a winter coat so the kids could have school shoes; when I felt trapped by the unrelenting demands: nursing the sick child, checking the homework, settling sibling squabbles, preparing the endless meals; when I felt resentful of their selfishness, their immaturity, their seeming ignorance of my "sacrifice." Probably all parents have such feelings now and then, but I think single parents are particularly susceptible to them. We feel so alone, so unappreciated.

But what I came to learn through observation of other single-parent households, and the developing relationships between mothers and their children, was that without a covenant concept, parents tend to shift their dependency onto their children, subtly bartering with them to fulfill their needs in exchange for taking care of theirs: the mother who never learned how to drive a car, expecting her son to take her to the grocery store, the doctor, clothes shopping; the widow who manipulates her daughter's concern for her, displaying just enough physical weakness to require she not leave home, yet not enough to warrant a doctor's attention and medical treatment; parents whose sole interest was child-centered, who are bitter and lonely when their children do marry and leave home, who are resentful of the time and effort they invested for so little return.

Learning to live with yourself is your responsibility, for the sake of the children while they are with you . . . for the sake of yourself when they are gone. Your children will grow and go whether you release them or not. Their love for you will not be measured by what they *owe* you.

Conversely, without covenant, single parenting can lead to neglect: the mother who packs her social calendar so full her children need appointments to see her, she stoutly proclaiming that "it's not the quantity of time that's important but the quality," offering neither; the mate-hungry widow who introduces her children to a succession of live-in lovers and weekend affairs, disregarding their need for emotional stability, dismissing their sexual curiosity; the self-pitying divorcée who fought the custody battle and won, now blaming her ex-husband and his missing support payments for her child's poor health, shabby dress, and poor school performance.

No. Parenting isn't contractual. You'll have to give much more than you can ever expect to get. You'll scratch and save to find the money for a snowsuit, or a prom dress, or soccer shoes. You'll turn down invitations to weekends at the beach cottage. You'll call in sick to the office or refuse a date with an attractive man because your little one has a raging fever and can't be left alone. That's parenting. And you aren't a martyr. You aren't your daughter's pal. You aren't your son's wife. You're a parent.

You will be my people: you are my children. I will lead you. I will meet your needs. I will seek what is good for you. I will give you my best self.

I will never let you go: YOU will let ME go. You will grow, you will love, you leave. I will not hold you. Yet I will never stop loving you.

How do you rebuild your child's trust after the marriage dies? Think covenant. It needn't be spoken, simply lived. Then you have a good chance of avoiding the two potentially dangerous paths of single parenting: living your life *through* your children; living your life in *spite* of your children. The one leads to neglect of your growth. The other to neglect of theirs.

Yes, you need to develop your own self. And, yes, your children need you. Think covenant. You can all "grow up" together.

SO YOU'RE A SINGLE PARENT?

Did you know that at least one fifth of all children under the age of eighteen are now living in a single-parent household? (In my community it's closer to one third.) You are not alone. And think of all the *functionally* single-parent households where Daddy leaves for work as the kids come down for breakfast and returns when they're ready for bed; where his personal hobbies consume his weekend.

If you're feeling sorry for yourself because your children don't have a live-in Daddy, and feeling inadequate to the task of parenting alone, take a look around you.

Who's nurturing these children, developing their character, overseeing their education, caring for their physical well-being? Mothers.

Who's at the teachers conferences? Who's arranging for the plumber to come, the doctor to call, the friends to visit? Mothers.

Self-pity wears many masks. The "poor single mother who just can't cope" is one. You don't have to wear it. You aren't so terribly special as you might like to believe. Millions of mothers have raised billions of children single-handedly. So can you.

The "broken home" indictment is too often exercised by teachers, neighbors, and even mothers and their children themselves, to lower their expectations of a single parent. Don't buy it. You can assure your children that there is no shame: "No, Shawn, you don't have to go up and down the street ringing doorbells. People will know in time. We're still our family." You can be alert for signs of embarrassment and self-pity in your children and make conscious efforts to have family projects that build their pride and self-esteem. And you can remind yourself that a far greater tragedy than single parenting is visited upon today's problem children—the tragedy of no parenting at all.

The only difference between you, a single parent, and many, many married parents is that you haven't a partner. And for most over-thirty-five mothers who are accustomed to the conventional pattern of a Daddy who *works for* the family and a Mommy who *takes care of* the family, that difference is simply that you have no one to tell you what to do, or approve of what you have already done. You have no one to blame when things go wrong and no one to applaud when things go well. You're a parent on your own.

And there's the rub. It's the responsibility that frightens. Not the tasks. When we were married we could duck behind the authority of our husbands, we could use the father *figure* to shield us from the consequences of our decisions. Now, we have no one to depend on. Others are dependent on us.

We separated in early October. The first months are a blur in my memory of letters and phone calls to my sisters, my brother, my mother; of confusing meetings with lawyers and awkward visits from "Dad." I raced to keep up with the children's day-to-day schedules of lunches, lessons, parties, and doctor appointments. I held a tight rein on my checkbook and as tight a rein on my emotions. Making it through each day without a crisis was sufficient. I feared the consequences of a drain on either.

It was a one-day-at-a-time existence. I was not yet ready to make decisions for our future and I made every effort to avoid being drawn into making commitments that, at the time, I was not at all sure I could keep. The children were concerned, I'm sure, and worried about their future, but I didn't yet know how to handle that. So I assumed a kind of "Girl Scout Camp leader" role, filling silences with platitudinous chatter, deflecting potentially emotional confrontations with cheerful proverbs and vacuous assurances.

"Of course, Daddy and I like each other. We just aren't able to live together, that's all."

"A stitch in time saves nine!"

"Why, really, nothing's going to change."

"Waste not, want not!"

"Aren't we having fun?"

• • •

Of course we weren't. Each of us was nursing our own private doubts about making life work without Dad—I most of all. Would I really be able to handle the responsibility?

Isn't it interesting how holidays become a special lens of the microscope through which we can observe a family, indeed many human relationships? No wonder there are so many suicides at holiday time . . . and family feuds . . . and tears.

Thanksgiving was, by mutual agreement, his holiday with the children. He called for them midmorning and took them to dinner with his sisters and their families in nearby Connecticut. I played "orphan" for a neighborhood family—the obligatory, needy guest who would appreciate the bounty of a family's "groaning board."

Thus, Thanksgiving passed us by with no particular trauma. My presence was missed at their traditional family gathering, the children said, and although I felt strangely alone at my neighbors, I accepted their felicitations and frankly enjoyed the respite from responsibility. We returned to our day-by-day doldrums.

Christmas loomed. (My turn.) Just hearing carols on the radio raised a lump in my throat. How could we possibly get through that maze of fourteen years of carefully crafted personal family traditions without their father? Could I alone lead us through the whole process of selecting a tree and trimming it, playing Santa Claus at midnight while the children pretended to sleep upstairs, waiting for me to fall into bed so they could sneak down in the early-morning light to see what Santa had brought? I didn't feel so. Could we go to the late-afternoon crèche service at church and join the pro-

cession of families to the manger scene, singing "O
Come, All Ye Faithful" as we marched hand in hand to
"Bethlehem," without their father? And afterward,
walk through the darkened streets to the village carol
sing, stand in the chill night air with our arms around
each other singing "Joy to the World!" without him?
And what on earth would we do all Christmas Day,
when the gifts had been opened, the wrappings disposed
of, turkey . . . chicken? . . . in the oven, the table set for
four?

No, I couldn't handle all that alone. I couldn't bear
the emotional burden of making Christmas happen. *My
God*, I thought, *it'll be a wake, not a celebration!*

I devised a dodge. I called my mother.

"I want to come home for Christmas," I announced,
and with rising excitement, put together the plan of how
I'd scrape together the air fare, make it my major gift to
the children, and we'd all fly home to Wisconsin. We'd
stay with Mother in town and then all of us would go
out to the country to my sister Carol and her family for
a good old-fashioned family Christmas.

Home. I was off the hook. Mother would take care. I
gave little heed to her quiet reminder that her apartment
was small (she'd left the big house on Dunbar Avenue
years ago when Dad died), that her arthritis wasn't *too*
bad, that she'd rent some cots to put us up. I heard only
her firm, "Of course," her warm, "I'll start getting
ready for you."

Carol, too, was warmly supportive. Of course, she
said, with all the in-laws, her children, cousins and
grandparents, it would be a full house, but, yes, do
come!

The children received the news with mild enthusiasm
and curiosity. They'd go along with whatever I sug-

gested. After all, this Christmas was new to them too. Ann asked to decorate the mantel so we could have some touch of Christmas spirit at home. We dragged the Christmas box out from under the cellar stairs. There, with the tree trimmings, ribbons, and candles were the five large red felt stockings that my mother had designed and hand-sewn for us many Christmases ago— our names inscribed on them. Wordlessly Ann selected our four, then carefully folded the one inscribed "Dad" and returned it gently to the box, saying, "He doesn't have a fireplace."

The four red stockings and a few evergreen boughs were all we had to remind us of Christmas in New York, and when I closed the door on them the morning of Christmas Eve, en route to the airport, I was as happy to be leaving them as I was to be running to the warmth and security of my idealized family Christmas at "home."

Mother greeted us at the door of her apartment, cane smartly decorated with a Christmas bow. I hadn't realized how far her arthritis had progressed, how difficult it was for her to get around. She positively glowed with love and excitement, hugging her grandchildren, squeezing my hand tightly, then ponderously maneuvering herself into her little kitchen for the cookies she had baked for the children.

We crowded around her tiny table, munching the ginger cookies that had been her hallmark of many Christmas seasons. My attention drifted as the spicy aroma stirred memories of the big white enamel table in the kitchen on Dunbar Avenue, Mother rolling out the dough, I shaping it with the assorted cookie cutters, snitching scraps and popping them in my mouth whenever she turned her back.

"The sofa opens up and you and I can sleep there."
She was chattering brightly. "And if we move that
table, we can put the cot there for Billy. Now, in the
study, if we put the desk against the wall, we can open
the daybed and the girls can sleep in there!"

We made up the beds. Mother's entire apartment
looked like one large mattress. I tucked the children
in, kissed them, whispering, "Merry Christmas" and
"We'll have a wonderful time tomorrow," then picked
my way around the pillows and blankets to my portion
of the sofa. Mother was already asleep, and I saw her
face was drawn and pale in the glow of the single light
we had left on in the bathroom.

Shawn threw up. *Airsickness—it'll pass,* I thought, as
I cleaned her up, then sat with her, trying to make her
comfortable and keep her quiet so as not to wake the
others. We slept.

David, Carol's husband, picked us up in the morning.
The large house, high on a snow-covered hill out in the
country, ten miles from town, was fairly bursting with
people—their five children, more grandmothers, in-
laws. The tree stood twenty feet high, touching the
cathedral ceiling of the living room, laden with the
handiwork of the children: popcorn and cranberry
strings and paper cut-outs. We added our gifts to the
mound that stretched halfway into the room, bundled
Shawn, still pale and weepy, into the corner of the sofa,
sent Billy and Ann off to play with their cousins, and
got the rundown on the day's activities from Carol. It
was apparent that she had been planning, organizing,
and working late into the night for weeks.

"First breakfast, then gifts, then buffet dinner, then
the cousins and some neighbors will be stopping by for
supper and dessert. Grandma, did you bring the

cookies? Patrick, you can set the table, now. Dan, try to round everyone up!'' She sparkled with enthusiasm and purpose. We basked in her affection and the attention of the crowd. And as we each settled into our assigned places for the sharing of gifts, I felt warmed by the light of their family's love exchanged, and their generous sharing of that light with us.

Ann threw up around noon. She rested on her cousin Bessie's bed. The children clearly were not feeling well and soon we are all transported back to Mother's pad, the echoing cries of ''Merry Christmas!'' accompanying us, yet the words carrying less meaning than they had a fortnight ago.

That evening, Billy got sick, Ann's fever rose, Shawn's subsided. Mother fixed us a pot of tea and we talked quietly at her table, in candlelight. She told me of how she'd found her little apartment, how well it suited her; of her daily routine, her friends, her work.

''It's satisfying, my dear,'' she said. ''And it's so wonderful to see you and the children. I wish I could do more for you. Dear, check Annie. See if her fever has gone down.''

She had asked no prying questions, offered no well-meaning advice. She had simply given as much as she was able to her daughter. Later as she slept on her piece of the sofa and I prowled about the apartment, stumbling over mattresses, a latter-day Florence Nightingale nursing her troops, I felt ashamed.

I'd run away from home that Christmas, dragging my children with me. My mother, a sixty-nine-year-old widow with crippling arthritis, and my older sister, mother of five and family hostess to scores of relatives, had opened their hearts and home to me and my children, picking up the slack when I dropped the reins of *my* responsibility as a mother. They did it willingly and with love, and as well as they could. But they couldn't give me what I knew then I had been seeking: a child's Christmas, free of responsibility. I had come home to Wisconsin to get from them what I had not been able to give to my own . . . childhood.

It was a simple flu of the twenty-four variety that felled the children. They recovered quickly. But their untimely illness served as an ironic underscore to our ill-timed visit. I walked with Ann and Shawn, now fully recovered, down the streets I had walked as a child—through the park, past Union School and the play-ground, down Maple, over to Dunbar Avenue.

"That's where I grew up," I said, as we looked up at the Victorian frame house on an embankment, freshly painted, a fat wreath on its door.

"Did you have good Christmases there?" Shawn asked.

"Mmm-hmm."

"I want to go home now," said Ann.

"So do I," said I.

And we did the next day. The greens had browned on the mantel, the empty stockings hung flat against the fireplace. We collapsed into the living room and stared at one another.

"Mom," said Billy (now fully recovered). He pulled himself up to his full thirteen-year, five-foot, five-inch height. "From now on, we want to spend Christmas at home. *Our* home."

The girls chimed in. "We love Grandma! Aunt Carol and Uncle Dave and all the kids are great! But we want to be home for Christmas!"

"So do I," I said.

We sat for a few minutes saying nothing, looking at the fireplace.

"Why did we go to Wisconsin?" Shawn asked.

"Because I was running away from home," I said flatly, looking them full in the face, no Girl Scout demeanor, no platitudes.

"Well. That's *dumb!*" exploded Billy. His jaw dropped and his eyes grew wide with shock at his own audacity. So did mine. We both gasped . . . then laughed. And then we were all laughing, and crying a little too, and I kept saying, "It's O.K., I'll be all right. . . . Oh, my . . . I'm your mother. . . . We're a family." And they were saying "Hey, Mom, it's O.K., we're together."

Maybe I needed to run away from parenting to find it. Maybe I needed to reexperience it in the lives of my mother and my sister. I'm not at all sure that the trip to Wisconsin was necessary for us, but I do know that sitting there in our own home four days after Christmas, my view of myself as a parent had changed; their view of me as their mother had altered. We were able to look at one another with honest eyes that were forgiving as well as loving. And I understood that a parent—married, single, divorced, widowed—gives not *tasks* but *self.* And the more responsible that self is—the more willing it is to take risks for the sake of its charges—the more valuable is the gift.

I think it was then that we began the creation of a new family. And when next Christmas rolled around and we discovered that the spring rains that had flooded the basement had gotten to the Christmas box and its contents had been destroyed by mold and mildew, we trimmed the tree with the children's toys, old jewelry, and whatnots. Ann's gift was four new personalized hand-sewn red felt stockings for the fireplace. We went to the services, I played Santa Claus, we invited the neighbors over on Christmas afternoon.

Our house felt warm and cozy—home. And the stockings, bulging with oranges, underwear, and candy bars, hung brilliant against the white brick fireplace—symbols of a new beginning.

A fat green wreath hung on our front door.

CHAPTER 9
Growing with Your Children

How shall we then live? It's a question that haunts each single mother as she contemplates the hostile gaze of her disappointed child, listens outside the bedroom door for sounds of crying, views with alarm the sudden development of facial tics, weight gain, gross disobedience, feels the tension in the home rising to explosive levels. From your new vantage point the days and years seem to stretch on forever. How shall we live them?

TELLING THE TRUTH

Cathy and Dan's marriage had *seemed* sound. They gave every appearance of being a well-adjusted couple, happy with each other and absolutely delighted with their only son, Danny. The three of them were a picture of family solidarity.

Said Cathy: "We believed in and practiced open communication. Danny was always able to give it to me right between the eyes—not in anger, just honestly. He felt free to let me know what he liked, what he didn't like. I encouraged that. I wanted to know what he was really feeling, not what I wanted to hear.

"So when Dan and I started to seek counseling, I told Danny that there was a possibility of separation, that our marriage might not work out, and that he'd be the first to know.

"Well, then we separated. After six months Danny said to me, 'You're never going to live with Dad again, are you?' and I said, 'You're right.' Just like that, I'd known it, but I hadn't said it.

"You know, it's the worst thing in the world to say or do something that hurts your child. That's what had kept me on the fence for so long. For years I had told Danny that while we weren't rich in money, our family was rich in other ways. That we had this lovely family life—blah, blah, blah—and then—I took the whole rug and pulled it out from under him. But I did believe that, terrible as it was, our separation would be *less* harmful to Danny in the long run.

"If you know, deep down, that one day it will be better . . . well, you have to hold on to that and tell the truth.

"Danny's reaction devastated me. He went into

shock and I had to call the doctor to give him a tranquilizer. He was on the floor like a little animal, shaking and crying. 'I had no idea! What did I do wrong? If I'm really good . . .'

"I could only keep saying to him: 'It had nothing to do with you. You are not responsible. Unfortunately, you're the guy in the middle who gets hurt. But I promise you, *you will get better*. It will get easier.'

"I was sick. In a way I was relieved because it was out in the open, but the pain of having to tell your child that he's not Beaver—you know, *Leave It to Beaver*—that was terrible. Every child wants its family to be 'normal,' to have its father live in the same house.

"At first, I felt so badly I just turned myself inside out—overindulged, overcompensated. I bent over backward in Danny's direction. I kept thinking, *He has all this anger in him. He needs reassuring.* I encouraged him to keep talking. He'd tell me how he was so ashamed at school. He wouldn't even go at first. And he said it was all my fault. I'd ruined his life. I let him talk . . . and go on about how I was the biggest creep in the world. That was O.K. for a while.

"But remember, I was out there slugging it out, trying to make as good a life as I could for us—working hard at my job in the city, yet being at his every baseball game, arranging my schedule so that if there was a concert in the morning, I'd be there. If there was a music lesson after school, I was there. Yet he was becoming more and more disobedient, angry, and insolent.

"One weekend I had to be in California on a business trip. I'd arranged everything for his care, his dad would be seeing him too. Well, I missed his baseball game. You know what he said? *I was a lousy rotten mother.* In those very words. That was too much. Yes, it was his

age (twelve can be rebellious), and yes, he was entitled
to blow up at me, and yes, he could hate me, that's his
choice, and he could say he hated me . . . but this was
unhealthy!

"Finally I said to him one night: 'You know, I'm not
perfect. I never said I was perfect. I'm sorry. If I could
have things right for you, I would. I couldn't and it is
really too bad. But things could be a lot worse.'

"What was the word I used? *Repression.* 'A little
repression is due here now. If you are going to grow up
with hang-ups, well, you are. But I am your mother and
I demand respect, and if we're going to live together,
you're going to do as I say. I am not going to have a
nervous breakdown because you have a tantrum!'

"That was a turning point. It was when I understood
that not only did I have an obligation to accept the painful truth from Danny's point of view, and to accept his
feelings, even his criticism, toward me, but I had an
obligation to be honest about myself, to myself and to
Danny. I *was, am* his mother. I owed him acknowledg-
ing that. I realized that if I didn't get control of our
household and exercise my responsibility, why, by the
time he was fourteen, where would I be? He'd be bigger
than I. He'd start beating me up!"

Cathy says she can laugh about it now, but it was
a serious and sobering turning point for her and for
Danny.

"Oh, he still feels free to tell me exactly how he feels.
And believe me, he does. But he will say to me every
now and then: 'Remember that night, that night when
you told me? And you would say, it will get easier, it
will get better? Mom, it has.' "

Cathy's husband was an alcoholic. She was concerned

for his well-being as well as Danny's. "They both saw me as the 'heavy' in the situation and I felt guilty and was bending over backward to accommodate their feelings.

"But once I took the lead, once Danny knew absolutely that I would stick my neck out for him, that I would make darned sure that he would indeed have his home, well, he developed positive courage to cope. Perhaps that comes from knowing that whatever he has to say—whether I agree, disagree, like it, don't like it—he's still loved. There's still a place for him. And I'll fight like a tiger to keep it and him secure.

"Looking back, I now think that children can sense who the more vulnerable parent is. That is the one they are more considerate of. Maybe it's the one who moves out who wears the white hat. And the one they live with wears the black. They lay all their anger and frustration at our feet because they know we can take it.

"That was a terrible first year. But I'm glad that I could somehow sweat it out."

Cathy found the healing role that truth plays with children. Danny's feelings were but one part of their relationship. At first, out of "guilt," she allowed his and denied her own. When, in desperation, she gave herself *back* to him—"I'm *not* perfect . . . I *am* your mother. . ."—a new dialogue was begun between parent and child.

"You know what I've become aware of? The power of grown-ups over children. The power of parents, of teachers. How it can be misused. It's within our power to choose to lie, to say something that will 'make it all right' for the present. It's within our power to deny their truth, for the present. We have to really be committed to truth—to finding it, to living it as best we can—to use our power for good.

"Danny's still putting the pieces back together. Maybe he'll never feel totally secure again, I mean in the old sense of family. But he's developing security in himself, becoming more direct and compassionate with his father, more understanding of me. I think we're on the way to a pretty good life!"

The power of grown-ups. Dependent women *do* shy from it. Power is so . . . so masculine . . . so accountable. Yet the fact is that as a single parent you have it. Whether you want it or not. How you use it is up to you.

GROWING INTO LEADERSHIP

Cathy picked up the reins the day she announced to Danny that, like it or not, she was his mother. And like it or not, as long as they were living together, she was calling the shots. I think that can be a psychologically difficult thing for women accustomed to dependency. Our experience was in nurturing and understanding. We learned early to accommodate Daddy's moods and conspired with Mom to get his approval. We used our children's father as a court of last resort when our efforts at understanding and persuasion failed with our own children.

Oh, sure, we had plenty of subconscious power—

manipulative power. History has well documented the "power behind the throne." Politicians rightly honor the "little woman without whom I could never have achieved so much"; and Mother's Day cards attest to the importance of Mom's love in the lives of her children.

That kind of power is sub rosa, not frontal. And if things don't turn out well, we are there to bind up the wounds of the fallen loved ones, or sigh, "I did as much as I could," or lend advice, encouragement, and understanding to the "other" to try again. *But we weren't/ aren't responsible.*

Single mothers have to learn to become leaders—conscious leaders. For your household to function comfortably, for your children to feel secure (they really know they aren't ready to call the shots), and for them to regain a sense of family pride that translates into self-esteem, your house needs a leader—a conscious leader. One who's willing to take risks, take blame, take charge.

Billy, Ann, and Shawn grew into their teen years. I found a better-paying job. Communication between us was open. We accomplished that. We worried through acne, diets, and dates. We cooked together, ate together, cleaned house together. We were four roommates. We were friends. And that was good.

But I hadn't reckoned with the pressures of the neighborhood, pressures of the street, pressures of the school yard. And as I was enjoying the friendship we were forging, even as we were becoming pals, buddies, and chums, there were things going on I knew not of.

How do I explain the shock of finding a heap of beer and liquor bottles in the basement, covered over by an old tarpaulin; the panic that propelled me up the stairs to the children's bedrooms, frantically searching for some clue to understanding what had been going on in my absence; the shame of picking up a diary and opening it, violating their trust, searching for evidence that they had violated mine; my despair at finding it—the documentation of parties in my absence, with the note: *I hope Mom doesn't find out.*

Shawn was the first home. She dashed up the stairs. I waited in the living room, listening to her steps, heard her stop. She would see the diary, open to the incriminating page, that I had angrily propped on her pillow. Then slow, heavy footsteps. She stood on the stairs. Her face was white.

"You read my diary."

"Yes."

"You shouldn't! You shouldn't ever . . ." She was screaming, frightened. Panicked. So was I.

I think I said something like, "You broke my trust." All I know is that I ran to my car and pulled away and was speeding out of town, onto a highway headed north.

I opened the car window to dry tears that wouldn't stop and I was hollering at the wind: "How could they do that to me? How could they betray me? They know how hard I'm working. I tried to be understanding of them. Why?" As I pictured the clandestine parties in *our house* . . . the booze . . . drugs? . . . I became so nauseous, I had to pull off the road. I rested my head on the steering wheel.

I must have slept, for the sun was near setting when I straightened up and looked about. I didn't know where I was. Some lights of a distant village were coming on and I drove toward them.

At a crossroads was a darkened church. It may have been abandoned. I don't know. But I got out of the car and sat on its steps, lit a cigarette, and tried to think.

On the one hand, they had broken a trust I had placed in them. They had let me down. And on the other hand, I was terribly ashamed that I had violated my own cardinal rule of privacy, the sanctity of a diary. Could I just keep heading north? A part of me really wanted to do that, to get away from any more hurt. To have no more responsibility. Yet Shawn's stricken face wouldn't leave me. "You're my people, kiddo," I muttered to myself, "and I'm not giving up on you yet."

The long drive back gave me plenty of time to think. Perhaps as I'd been focusing on my own need to grow, shoring up my own confidence in the world of work, I'd been ducking the additional job of being a leader to my children. I'd been counting on love and understanding to see us through. When it wasn't there, I'd bolted.

They were seated on the sofa. A mass of spaghetti was congealed in a pot on the stove. The table was set. No one had eaten.

"Where have you been?" Billy asked.

Looking at the three of them—Ann and Shawn, with their swollen eyes and blotchy cheeks, Billy, stern and pale—I could only whisper, "I left you." And Shawn shuddered. "You can't do that. What would we do without you?" And I said: "I came back. I'm your mother." And then we were all crying and I said that we'd broken each other's trust and that we had to start from scratch but we could do it.

I took a deep breath and said: "This is our home. And we are going to have rules to protect it. And you are my children and I am going to fight tooth and nail to protect you. If you don't like it, that's tough. I'm your mother and I'm not going to give up. Ever. I love you too much. Now then.''

I got a yellow pad and we all sat around the dining room table. At the top of the pad I wrote: *Our Family Covenant.* Then we discussed those things we valued that made our home precious to us, and what it was we felt we had a right to expect of each other. And I wrote:

Because we are a family and because we want to live together in this house, we agree:

1. *No parties without Mom's O.K.*
2. *We don't want people on drugs in our house.*
3. *Drunk grown-ups aren't welcome either.*

We went on in that fashion, talking and writing, well into the morning. We signed the paper and I taped it to the refrigerator door. It stayed there for several weeks although we never had to refer to it again. Then I took it down, tattered and finger-marked, and folded it away in the drawer with the baby pictures—a memento, for me, of the day I grew up, grew from ''Mom'' to ''Parent.''

Parenting, I found out, is more than caring and comforting. It's also teaching and leading. Billy said later: ''We were waiting for you to take charge. We're proud of you. And we're proud of our family, too.''

Thank God, they waited for me.

CHAPTER 10
Men!

Betty found her old boyfriend. He was ten years older than she, over sixty, still a bachelor. He'd always loved her, he said, and had never met a woman who equaled her. He said his responsibilities of caring for his mother and his business had filled his years quite satisfactorily. That Betty should reappear in his life was, he said, truly a miracle. His mother had just died, he was making plans for his retirement, he loved Betty. What could be more perfect?

That his home was two thousand miles from Betty's was awkward, of course. But eventually they could work something out. Betty was sure of that. She wallowed in his attention, albeit long distance.

"We had little code signals for calling each other every day. I lived for those calls. I organized my day around them. The anticipation of hearing his kind voice on the telephone was so delicious. I'd rush home from work and wait, and wait. I was like a junkie. I had to get my fix. We'd whisper sweet things to each other. I felt so . . . so . . . young and attractive . . . so lovable.

"I became dependent on his confirming my acceptability as a woman. I was like a teenager asking Daddy if my dress was pretty. Maybe that's what he really was to me—Daddy. I was so insecure, so unsure of myself, that I sought—needed—some older, wiser man's approval and acceptance.

"We went on that way for a couple of months. And when I finally realized that he was not going to marry me—rescue me, really—I literally thought I was going to die. The pain was far worse than any pain I'd felt when my marriage broke up. And I thought I was experiencing love. But now I know it wasn't. It was addiction—emotional addiction. We didn't even know each other! But I was so grateful for his attention, so hooked on the *feeling* of romance, that I called it love.

"Like any addictive substance, it kept me from seeing the truth. It let me avoid coping with living with myself and learning to like myself.

"Maybe newly single women are particularly vulnerable. Maybe we unconsciously seek emotional addiction as a kind of delaying tactic. Maybe we really need it for a short period of time. And that's O.K. For it was after that affair that I began to grow.

"He returned my letters when he broke it off. Recently I took them out to read. Sad little musings . . . tentative gropings . . . they hadn't been letters to him, I realized. They had been letters to me. I'd used him to get to know myself, that was all.

"He's married someone else now and so have I. I'm content, comfortable, and happy—with me and with my husband. I sincerely hope my old boyfriend is happy too. But I'm awfully glad I didn't marry him. When my addiction wore off, why, we would have had nothing!''

DON'T MARRY THE FIRST ONE!

I know. He's so sensitive. He's so gentle. He makes you feel like a girl again. He's probably a good deal older than you—or a bit younger. And he's not like those *other* men. He's strong—or he needs you. Before you go racing off to the altar, ask yourself: who *is* he really like? Your father? Your teenage boyfriend? What is he really doing for you? And what are you doing for (or to) yourself?

A new dependent relationship is so seductive. And you are so particularly vulnerable to it now. It would be so much easier to be Daddy's little girl or a carefree teenager again. So restful to make a soporific of infatuation and sleep your cares away. The only problem is: you wake up. And you're just a little bit older. You still don't know who you are, and you still haven't learned to live with yourself. There's a strong chance that he'll die before you do and you'll be right back where you are right now—formerly married. Formerly married, dependent, and with less time and less courage to learn to cope with your remaining years.

Lois got married. Right away.
"I was feeling like such a failure after my divorce.

Remember, my father had walked out on me when I was little and I guess I'd always harbored some feelings of inadequacy. Then, when Bob left, I was convinced of it.

"Jim was young. He was gorgeous. He taught me to dance. Infatuation? I was delirious! He needed me, he said, and oh, boy! did I need to be needed. Some little part of me hesitated to marry so quickly, but I was so breathless with that feeling of being *chosen,* so anxious that I would lose him and his attention, that I married him.

"Well, our marriage fell right into the pattern of my previous one. Jim was no different from Bob—*I* was no different. I was the same insecure, dependent girl I'd always been, trying to adapt my talents, my interests, my personality, to suit his needs . . . to gain his approval. And Jim used it to mask his own feelings of inadequacy in much the same way Bob had. And it didn't work. It couldn't work. How could we be for each other what we weren't for ourselves?

"I'm beginning to understand all this now, but, of course, I didn't know at the time. We *don't* know. We don't know who we are until we take the time to find out. We probably can't know our reasons for being attracted to a particular person right after we're divorced or widowed. But we can know that *there are reasons*. And they are rooted much more deeply in our past—not our future.

"Infatuation? Sure. Maybe it will happen again. But I know now that it isn't love. And I'm going to learn from it, grow through it, and *not* marry it!"

Gloria feels comfortable with an older man who's very kind to her.

"I'm just not interested in that whole competition

game of the young singles. I feel too threatened, too vulnerable. Probably my friend is some kind of father figure. But that's all right, for now. I won't get really serious, though. I'd never marry him!''

Ann found gaiety and laughter with a charming "gentleman." "It was great fun for a while and I needed that. But I found out he was an alcoholic, so . . .''

I tumbled for a man in the theater group. He was older, wiser than I (I thought). He even *looked* like my father. During my addictive phase, I'm embarrassed to confess, I actually talked baby talk to him. (Now there's a father figure!) But as I became more self-confident, he withdrew. When I woke up, I saw that I had endowed this nice man with all sorts of qualities he didn't possess. He wasn't nearly as wise and strong as I'd imagined. No one could be. He was just a nice man with whom I had little in common.

Emotional vulnerability and infatuation. They seem to go hand in hand. Be patient. Heed Lois' advice. Don't marry when they have you in their grip.

WHERE THE BOYS ARE

She called for me that Friday evening around seven. The meeting didn't start until eight, she said, but it would be more fun if we got there early. That way we could size up the guys.

What was I doing, racing along the New England Thruway toward Connecticut with this other middle-aged woman at the wheel, chattering about what fun I'd soon be having?

Well, I'd decided that I owed it to myself to follow the advice of the columnists. I owed it to myself to check out a singles group. I was leery. I'd never been much of a joiner. But I'd had a long talk with myself and concluded that one time would be, at the very least, educational. Why knock it before I tried it?

We walked into a cavernous church hall already beginning to fill up with men and women of a certain age. Two burly men flanked me as I affixed my name tag to my blouse. One brought me coffee. "It's wine and cheese after," whispered my friend. Soon we were engulfed in a sea of bodies in motion. "Mingle" must have been the password, as hearty "Hi how are yuh's" whizzed by. Eyeballs were in perpetual motion, checking each new arrival. I decided to stand in one place. Make it easier on their eyes.

"First time here, Marilyn?"

"Uh, yes."

"Oh, that's great, simply great. You'll love it! I've been coming for over five years. Wouldn't miss it for anything!"

He was perhaps in his middle forties, porky, buttons of his flowered sport shirt straining over his barrel belly.

"Really great talking to you," he said as he moved on to a group of suited suburbanite ladies, slapped one on the back, gave them all a "Hi how are yuh" and moved on again. Everyone was moving.

A bell rang and discussion time was announced. We flocked to the exit, then downstairs to assigned classrooms, ten or twelve of us in each room. Perched on chairs designed for four-year-olds, knees to chins, the group discussed: "Communication: How Can I Tell You What I Really Feel?" Apparently a topic assigned by the national chapter. Each was eager to tell his story—of abuse, of missed alimony, of loneliness, of complicated will and trust arrangements, of adultery and love affairs.

One woman, visibly pained, told of her shock at discovering her husband's infidelity. She was obviously a newcomer to this scene and needed to spill it out. The rest squirmed. They'd been through that "stuff" two, three, even five years ago. But she seemed relieved to be able to talk, and the lay leader listened sympathetically.

Talk-time over, we returned to the hall, tables now holding jugs of wine and trays of cheese.

"Porky" returned to my elbow. "You're really very attractive, Marilyn," he breathed at me.

"Thank you," I said.

"Want to go dancing after this?" he asked.

"Oh, no, I came with a friend. Tell me," I said, trying to change the subject. "These people seem to be making a career of their divorces. Don't they ever talk about anything else?"

He looked puzzled. "But that's what we're here for. To help them talk about it."

"Yeah, that's fine, initially. But for five years? How long have you been divorced?"

He shrugged. "Oh, I'm married. You see, my wife doesn't understand my need to go out and have some fun. So I come here. I meet lots of lovely ladies here." He grinned.

I was furious. I'm still furious. That even one creep

like "Porky" could prey on emotionally defenseless women and get away with it. And I was depressed. Depressed that so many formerly married people's lives are stuck at that breaking-apart point and never get put back together.

Did I meet men that night? Certainly I didn't meet men who had compelling interests in world affairs or music or art or their careers. I didn't meet men who were too busy creating a new life to waste time on the old. I met boys. Narcissistic little boys in grown men's clothes. Fifty-year-old boys ogling similar girls. And one creep.

Don't get me wrong. The newcomer, I believe, found solace and perhaps a bit of courage in the commonality of the group. And surely there are terrific men and women who attend such meetings to find their bearings and to break out of the self-imposed solitary confinement that often accompanies divorce and widowhood. That's healthy.

But I think they must move on, as all of us must—on to new activities and associations that reflect present interests, hobbies, and concerns. I only wonder about those who stay.

Where else will you find boys? At any bar after six o'clock in the evening. They may look like men in their well-cut business suits, with their attaché cases and Rolex watches. But if they're not on their way to the theater, or meeting some friends for dinner, or going home, or going anyplace—in other words, if they are simply there, night after night—you can be sure that they're boys. Boys who haven't learned to live with themselves, and are filling their empty time with booze-induced bravado. That may seem a harsh indictment, but if you are really working at developing your interests, and learning how to enjoy your own life, wouldn't you like to share it with a man who's doing that, too?

"Why is it," said Barbara, "that the guys I meet at singles bars will take me to concerts and movies and art galleries—wherever I want to go—as long as we're just dating? As soon as I get 'hooked' and our relationship starts getting serious, they're not interested in those things anymore. I feel like I've been seduced!"

She probably has been seduced—emotionally and intellectually. Boys will do that. Men don't.

WHERE THE MEN ARE

"Believe me," said Cathy, "I wasn't looking. Oh, sure, after Dan left I did go through a period of adjusting to the empty house, especially when our son, Danny, was spending a weekend with him. It was odd because I'd always *stolen* private time away from them when they were home. I used to tell myself, 'If I could only have more time to myself, I'd really get such and such a task done.' Well, when I was alone, I found out that those tasks didn't take so much time after all, and I wanted to get out of the house! So single friends, and couples, too, would include me in their parties—I saw to that—and I'd meet guys, and sometimes we'd go to dinner or a movie. But I paid them no attention, really. I was just very busy being very busy.

"Then I settled down. I threw myself into my work, my home, Danny. Ron was the guy I'd grab a hamburger with and trade shop gossip. When the pressure at the agency was heavy I could count on him to make me laugh. But we were just plain friends. We'd known each other for years.

"One particular day Ron came into the office, back from a business trip, and I realized how much I had missed him. And I said: 'Ron, I really missed you. I'm so glad you're back!'

"He looked a little amazed, and he said: 'I really missed you, too, Cathy. We'll have to talk about this.'

"And now we're getting married! We like each other. We always have. And we love each other. We have so much life to share. And we can laugh together. Isn't that incredible? I never wanted to get married again. Now look at me!"

How do you meet men? Interesting men? Probably when you're not looking. And where you're not looking. They're the hardworking guys down the hall, the volunteers at the hospital, the students in night school, the audience at the play you loved, the stamp collectors, dog trainers, golfers, tennis players, joggers, and music lovers who people your life.

Dates don't materialize on doorsteps. Interesting men don't, either. They're too busy living interesting lives. As Cathy said: "He's the guy I can talk shop with. He's the guy I laugh with."

Betty met Frank at a church fund-raising meeting. Ann became friends with Larry as they were hammering out an artist's contract. Bruce invited me to the theater as I waited with friends for a table at a restaurant in the theater district. Were we looking for them? No. I think we were too busy. They might have become co-workers. They might have become friends. That they became interesting husbands and lovers grew from living experiences into living relationships.

WHAT'S YOUR NEED?

I know. "All the good ones are married."

If they are over thirty-five and are great husbands and lovers, they're probably still married and will remain so until she dies. If they're divorced, you wonder *why?* If they never married, you wonder *why?* You're wary of getting involved with a guy with heavy hang-ups and you don't want to repeat the problems of your former marriage. The men you meet are difficult, gay, or married.

Now's a good time to ask yourself: *What is it I really need?* If it's companionship, money, social life, security, prestige, love and respect, aren't you actually finding these things in many different people as you pursue your interests, develop your talents, and open your heart as well as your door to those who share your life? You may not be finding all your needs met by *one single available man*. But do you have to?

So many women complain about not being able to

find "a man," while all around them, giving them support and love, are the great people who are constantly enriching their lives in special, singular ways.

There's nothing wrong with you or your life if you don't happen to meet Mr. Right. A good man nowadays *is* hard to find: *most* of the good ones *are* married. That's just the way it is. But a man, *just* a man—a male person, one of those boys—believe me, he's available. Do you really need him?

CHAPTER 11
Making Your Living

So you're finding emotional, social, and spiritual security. That's living. Now, do you have the financial support to maintain it? That's *making* a living. You don't need to be rich and famous. You don't have to be a captain of industry or a torchbearer for women in business. You don't have to have a "fulfilling" career. But capital depreciates, the cost-of-living escalates, child support ends, and even alimony payers die. If you're contemplating a long and reasonably happy life, you'll want to be able to support it. And as Janet said, "I finally realized that if I were to continue living as I am, I'd be eating cat food when I'm sixty!"

Now's the time to take stock of your financial situation. Do you have health insurance? One broken leg could wipe out all your savings. What's your Social

Security status? Can you earn more money now to increase your future benefits? To what extent is your lifestyle being maintained by child-support payments? Could you live in the style to which you've become accustomed without them?

It's tempting to consider that somehow someone will take care of you and keep you from harm, that your Daddy's estate or your grown children will always provide. City shelters are full of women who thought so. Bag ladies sleep in doorways. We read newspaper stories of "crazy ladies" in tumbledown mansions who die of malnutrition. Perhaps they, like Scarlett O'Hara, thought they'd "think about it tomorrow." Tomorrow's too late. Think about it now. Think about it while you still have your health and your wits.

You are the only person who can make (create) your own living. But you can create it only from the substances of what you have. If you can't pay, you can't play.

Perhaps you already have a career direction. Now you'll want to evaluate what the loss of your former husband's income will mean to you in terms of securing your future.

Lois had always been committed to her writing projects. They satisfied her creative bent. But she'd never evaluated her work in simple financial terms. Her income from it had been absorbed into the "family pot."

"I discovered I was *more* valuable than I'd thought— or than my husband had led me to believe. I'd been playing at my work. Oh, I took it seriously for creative reasons, but never for financial ones. When I found out that I'd been carrying the larger share of our expenses, I was shocked. And then, because we're in a community property state, when I had to use my only personal savings to pay off his bad debts, I was doubly shocked.

"So I started off living alone dead broke. But for the first time in my life I saw myself as my own caretaker. And I determined then that never, never again would I surrender the responsibility for my upkeep to someone else. It's going to take me at least three years to get where I want to be—financially secure. And I'm working harder, more creatively than I ever have, to get there.

"Do you know how important my work is to me now? Why, it gives me reason to bound out of bed in the morning. I'm so proud of me! I'm learning about investments. I'm plotting my future. I'm in control of what I have. It's the most satisfying experience of my life."

Lois is beginning to get a taste of the power that comes with financial responsibility—and she's enjoying it. Ann, too, tasted it and liked it. When her husband, Alan, died, he left Ann with a respectable portfolio of investments.

"He'd always made the financial decisions for the two of us, and he did quite well. When he died, I was tempted to just abdicate any responsibility and turn all of it over to the banks. Then I started eavesdropping on the conversations of businessmen—You know, 'Watch such and such a stock, it's got good growth potential,' and I began reading the financial pages in the papers, and reading about investments, and asking questions. I made some conservative buys and watched them perform. Not bad, I thought. That was a few years ago, and now I'm pretty well off. It's interesting—with my business, which I love, and my investments, which are very secure, I don't feel a need to marry a man for financial security. That is wonderfully freeing. I can love. I can give. I don't have to take."

Of course, it's easier to secure your future if you have a financial base to start with. But even if you don't, if you have work experience that can be developed, you can start building your financial independence.

Cathy had had a successful advertising career before she married Dan. Both her parents had died by the time she was seventeen years old, and as surrogate parent to her younger brothers, she learned early the necessity of making a living and making do.

"Dan and I got married in the middle '60s. And when Danny was born, I really cut back on my career. Oh, I still kept my finger in the business with a little part-time work. I made enough money to meet personal needs like clothes, or a cleaning lady. But we lived on Dan's income.

"Then came the divorce. I had vowed to myself and to Danny that I would do everything possible to keep up our way of life—same school, same house, and all. What a shock! I can say now that we can't really know the kinds of pressures our husbands had to bear. We can't really know until we walk in their shoes. The anxiety of 'Will I have enough money to pay the mortgage?' And 'What if someone gets sick?' I realize now how many guys live with that—unquestioningly. They pull up their socks every day, go out there to the marketplace, do the best they can, and then they're berated for not being sensitive. Maybe they would rather have stayed home and let us slug it out for a while!

"I'll say this: I respect work now—all work. I take it very seriously. I found a full-time responsibility that pays me enough money to keep things going. I'm in charge of my life because I've *earned* the right to be. Shouldn't we all?''

Yes, we probably should. And the light of self-esteem that shines from these women's eyes confirms it.

To know we can take care of ourselves—to be able to pay for how we play—seems to be that last definitive step we have to take before we can truly respect ourselves and enjoy our own company. Until then, we're on the dole, relying on the alimony-check writer, the nameless, faceless trust officer or insurance adjuster, or the largesse of Daddy. That's living dependently, not *making* a living and creating a life.

PLANNING AHEAD

But what if the children are young and need your nurturing? Or you can't afford to pay for child care? Mothering is honorable work. Necessary and important work. You and your children are fortunate if you have access to funds that will support you through your mothering years. Just remember—those years will end, as will the support. That which you postpone now, you'll face later: how to make your own living.

If you're not ready to enter the work force, there are things you can do now to prepare yourself. Typing classes will give you a rudimentary office skill. No, you needn't feel that you'll be sentenced to a secretarial job just because you can type. Barbara got her typing up to forty-five words a minute, then registered with an employment agency for office temporaries. She took assignments as her family's schedule allowed, using each one as an opportunity to learn firsthand the workings of local business establishments, the job opportunities that might exist, and her compatibility with the various industries.

"How would I have known that the college needs a fund raiser, and that one company has a whole department devoted to community relations? It will still be several years before I can work full time, but I'm glad I can use these years to find out about possibilities and prepare myself."

There are career-planning courses, college degree programs, temporary and part-time jobs. All can be windows to the working world through which you can see where you might fit someday. Take a look.

REEVALUATING YOUR ABILITIES

Just because you haven't *earned* your living doesn't mean you haven't developed the skills to do it. The following are excerpts from résumés of late-blooming career women:

Directed annual campaign for United Fund. Through intensive use of publicity and promotion materials (samples attached), exceeded goal by 20 percent.

Director of hospital volunteer services program. Responsible for the performance of twenty-five volunteers; scheduling, assignments, follow-up.

As chairman of school board, was responsible for a budget of $1 million. Overseer of faculty selection. Directed public meetings. Prepared and designed annual reports.

The above, all community service volunteer activities, required skills of management, communication, finance, and public relations—skills that are valued in the working world, skills that employers are willing to pay money for.

Take another look at your volunteer work. What have you been doing these past years? What can you do these next years to develop yourself professionally? Take this time of your life seriously and use it to develop those abilities which can be translated into business skills. You'll have at least one leg up the ladder toward the world of work, and you'll be several rungs above the women who are using their spare time playing bridge, watching soap operas, and shopping. Your credentials can be impressive if you consciously work at developing them.

WORKING

That first serious job when you are actually making your own living can be scary. It's not like that time after college when you and a couple of roommates got jobs in the city, spent all your money on clothes, and then quit to get married and have babies. It's not like the interesting little part-time job you had that time when money was tight and you helped your husband by earning your own pin money. No. Now you're in the big time. It isn't play anymore. It's work.

Betty says she was so nervous when she got her job at the newspaper, her hands would rattle on the typewriter keyboard.

"My work was important and I had to produce. Having a 'great personality' just wasn't enough. Do you know, I wore nothing but beige and gray that first year! I was so afraid I'd be noticed . . . and be fired. It was grim. It took me over a year to trust my ability. During that time I just worked very carefully to check for mistakes, and I acted *as if* I belonged there. Eventually I guess I grew into the role, because now I wouldn't give up my work for anything!"

Role-playing does help. You won't ease your feelings of insecurity if you look like a housewife on Wall Street, and you won't arouse confidence in your boss if you act like her daughter, his wife, or their mother. If you practice being professional, and act *as if* you know what you're doing (and you *do* or you wouldn't have gotten the job), you'll discover that you can grow into the role and be comfortable in it.

And the money you make—the money whose steward

you now are—is your own, paid in exchange for your ability and effort. It's not an allowance. You earned it.

Many years ago, when my children were young, a doctor whom I considered very wise, Franz Winkler, spoke to me about his theory of adult life stages.

"You have your *reproductive* stage," he said with a nod of approval. "You have babies, you build your nest, you care for the family. That's good. But then you must move into the *productive* stage. You must grow up. If not?" He shrugged. "Early senility."

Why make your own living? Maybe for the self-esteem that grows as you manage your own affairs: maybe for the quiet maturity that develops as you consider the stewardship of your resources; and maybe, just maybe, to avoid a *second* childhood. One dependent life is enough for any woman. Do you really want another?

CHAPTER 12
Living Grown-up

As a child I loved to read. The only comfortable chair for reading, in our house on Dunbar Avenue, was what was referred to as "your father's chair." It was a big overstuffed armchair. A brass floorlamp stood behind it and a table ample enough to hold his newspapers and coffee was beside it. It was a cozy, inviting setting. I could sit cross-legged in the chair, cushioned by the broad armrests, or scrunch into one corner and dangle my feet over them.

When I got home after school and found no one home, I'd read there, until that moment when I'd hear his key in the lock and his footsteps in the hall. Then I'd leap from the chair, hide my book under the papers and start straightening up the room, fluffing sofa pillows and dusting tabletops. I'd greet him, he would sit in his chair, and I'd move into the kitchen if chores were to be done, or up to my room to do my homework.

I don't believe he knew what I was doing. I didn't know why, myself. We never discussed it. No one had ever said, "You may not sit in your father's chair." I simply deferred to him. I felt just a little bit naughty for being "selfish"—a little bit fearful of his finding me out. Maybe it was appropriate behavior for a young girl who feared her father's disapproval and sought to please him and make him comfortable. I don't know.

But I *do* know that I was dependent. Children are. But I think that child-rooted sense of the necessity of deferring to men persisted into my adult life in inappropriate ways. Even though they were not stronger, or brighter, or more powerful than I, *feeling* dependent on them was more comfortable than *being* independent.

Oh, to what lengths will some women go to hold on to that feeling! Avoiding personal success, feigning fascination with subjects that don't interest, repressing personal opinions, *stealing* time for personal pleasures —that's dependent living; childlike living and inappropriate for grown-ups. When you're grown-up, it isn't really comfortable.

"What is so great about living with yourself as a grown-up human being," says Betty, "is that when you do meet someone, you have something to give—not give up.

"I knew I could never give up what I've worked so hard to get—my job, my values, friends, activities, even my lifestyle. They all add up to who I am. And I like me.

"When I met Frank, my first thought was, 'Oh-oh. What's he going to expect from me?' Well, I found out,

amazingly, that all he expected was for me to be myself
—what I'd become and what I was becoming.

"If we'd met back when I was still feeling dependent
and needy, why, I'd have nothing of myself to share with
him—no ideas, no convictions, no point of view. Oh, I
could have done his laundry and fixed his meals. But so
could have a housekeeper. Now we're friends. He's a
man who enjoys me as a person as I do him. Besides, he
likes doing his own laundry.

Friends. Living grown-up is living with friends . . .
and your *best friend* is yourself. You'll enjoy your life
with yourself as you create it, and you'll appreciate the
contribution that others can bring to it.

It's not a temporary phase, lasting only as long as
you're single. It lasts forever, whether you marry again
or not.

Now, I can delight in coming home from work, curl-
ing up in my own easy chair, and reading a book. And if
I hear a key in the lock, or the footsteps of someone I
love in the hall, I don't have to jump up. When we grow
up we put away childish things.

Epilogue

It was a beautiful night in early June. And we were having a party. We had hatched the idea of it several weeks prior with lots of phone calls, list-making, and letter-writing. Billy had just graduated from college. Ann would be starting her junior year. Shawn would be a freshman in the fall. All three would be away for the summer, working. This one weekend was all we would have together as a family.

Ann had roasted a turkey. Shawn had arranged platters of hors d'oeuvres. Billy had shopped for the paper goods, set out ice and drinks. We had scrubbed down the patio and set out candles and lanterns on the tables and fence posts.

Now the four of us stood on the back porch: Billy, twenty-two, weighing the pros and cons of business vs.

academia; Ann, twenty, dreaming of Russian studies in Moscow; Shawn, eighteen, eager to begin the serious study of art; I forty-five and content.

Our guests were the reason for the party. Each had, in some way, shared in our growing up, accompanied at least one of us along the way. The teacher who gave Ann extra encouragement, the theater people who gave me confidence, the baby-sitters, neighbors, classmates, co-workers, teachers, and friends who had taught us the meaning of grace. This was our opportunity to thank them for their countless unearned gifts of love—a hot meal when I was sick, a front-porch conversation, a kind word, a handhold—grace in abundance.

The guests arrived. The children moved to greet them. *Let the celebrations begin,* I mused. *We've made it, so far.*

Bruce joined me on the porch. Bruce. Writer, companion, friend.

"So far," I said to him as we watched their three figures in the flickering candlelight—meeting, separating, merging, then disappearing into the shadows.

Nine years ago could I have known, I wondered, what lay in store for me when I had stood on this very spot and watched my old life leave? Probably not. Would I have chosen it? Probably not. Yet now I knew that, however arduous, the destination was worth the trip. The lessons learned had strengthened me for the next leg of my journey, wherever it might lead.

Three young adults were embarking on three separate paths. I would, and could, walk a fourth. And my closest companion, my surest guide, would be myself. If another's path paralleled mine, it would be pleasant; if not, I'd still enjoy the journey.

We were not together again until Christmas. We sang

carols in the village streets, hung the little toys and
bibelots on the tree, welcomed the neighbors on Christmas afternoon. The mantel was covered with evergreens
and from it hung the bright-red stockings—Mom, Billy,
Ann, Shawn . . . Bruce. Ann had sewn it for him as her
gift to him, welcoming him into the family. We would
be married in the month.

No, we can't know where paths will lead us. Even
now I don't. But I do know I'd rather walk than be carried, I'd rather love than need. People who need people
aren't really very lucky. People who love people are.